TORCH BIBLE

The Gospe

SAIN

THE GOSPEL ACCORDING TO

SAINT LUKE

W. R. F. BROWNING

SCM PRESS LTD

334 00940 5

First published 1960
by SCM Press Ltd
58 Bloomsbury Street London WC1
Revised edition 1972
Fourth impression 1977

Printed in Great Britain by
Fletcher & Son Ltd, Norwich

CONTENTS

XIV

XV

XVI

XVII

XVIII

XIX

XX

XXI

XXII

XXIII

XXIV

PREFACE

When this book was first published, in 1960, it represented an attempt to introduce the general reader to Redaction Criticism, i.e. the study of each of the Gospels as a whole instead of the atomistic method of Form Criticism. Redaction Criticism maintains that the evangelists were no mere editors or compilers; each had his own distinctive theological point of view which he imposed on the material that he inherited from predecessors or from oral tradition. The writings of A. M. Farrer and R. H. Lightfoot had familiarised English-speaking students with the general principles of the new discipline, but the name Redaction Criticism only became established later when translations of a new generation of German scholarship became available. (One or two of these books are listed in the bibliography, p. 33.)

The commentary also asserted in 1960 that there was as yet no solution to 'the synoptic problem' (What material was inherited by which evangelist? How account for the large quantity held in common by Matthew, Mark and Luke?) and it adopted the minority view that Luke knew both Mark and Matthew. This was at the time a bit rash; most scholars held that the reason why Matthew and Luke had so many sentences in common which obviously did not derive from Mark was because they had access to another document, or source of information ('Q'); and this commentary was criticised for 'disregarding the patient work of scientific study'. However, twelve years later the use of the source Q by Matthew and Luke and even the priority of Mark are generally admitted to be wide open issues, and I do not feel inclined to revise my brief references to the literary question.

W. R. F. BROWNING

INTRODUCTION

THE GOSPELS

There are at least four common views about what the Gospels are.

(1) Conservative scholars see them as uncomplicated accounts of what actually happened, and the fact of their divine inspiration guarantees the accuracy which the writers themselves claim. Luke's shepherds really did visit the infant Jesus at Bethlehem, because a real angel told them to do so; the veil of the Temple was literally torn in two; and after the Ascension the earth was a few stones lighter. Doubtless Matthew and Luke made use of Mark, but if there are any apparent discrepancies, one should not talk about 'mistakes' or 'corrections'. Matthew asserts that two demoniacs met the Lord, while Luke follows Mark in mentioning only the *one* who was more violent and whose cure was specially striking. If a saying of Jesus is given by Matthew and by Luke in totally different contexts, both are right. 'There is no reason why weighty words of this nature should not have been spoken on several occasions' (W. F. Arndt, Commentary on Luke).

(2) The synoptic Gospels can be regarded as the records of historical events, which when subjected to a thorough critical examination, can be reliably assessed for their accuracy. The result, though much must be relegated to the category of legend, doctrinal accretion etc., nevertheless gives us a fair picture of what Jesus said, of his psychological development, and the main course of his ministry. The Gospels, though not accurate in the sense of the for-

mer view, mean what they say and do not possess any hidden meaning.

(3) Much more sceptical is the view of some Christian scholars of the Form Critical School that the Gospels are better evidence for the life of the Church, in which and for which they were all composed, than for the life of Jesus which they purport to describe. The paragraphs and chapters of the Gospels form but a random pattern and have only been preserved at all because of the value they had for the Church, and in the course of transmission they were adapted to the Church's needs. It is only when some story seems to have no possible relevance to the life of the Church that there is sound evidence of historicity. Thus out of more than six hundred pages of his magisterial *Theology of the New Testament* (ET vol. I 1952, vol. II 1955) Dr Rudolf Bultmann devoted only forty to Jesus, who has been regarded by Bultmann, consistently over a period of thirty years as a NT scholar, as a mere Jewish rabbi of no particular distinction. A vigorous debate has continued in German theological circles, but it should be said that for Bultmann himself this historical scepticism was a gain rather than a loss for Christian faith, which, he maintained, ought not to be supported by worldly techniques of research. Moreover, radical NT criticism delivers us from antiquarian notions and from a false metaphysic, e.g. from the notion of a divine being who 'came down from heaven' and who proceeded in the course of an encounter with Satan and other demonic powers to interfere with the processes of nature—all of which presupposes a cosmology such as no educated man in the western world accepts. But thus liberated, modern technological man can reconsider what the Gospel does mean for Christian believers, when it is reinterpreted in the modern idiom, which, in Bultmann's view, is available in modern existentialism. And as a matter of fact there are traces within the NT, especially in St Paul's epistles, of

just this way of thinking. Romans 7 is an example of how St Paul moves from the cosmic realm to the personal history of an individual.

Each of these three points of view has immense difficulties. The *first* does not take into account the range of differences between the Gospels both in the facts that are mentioned and the way they are recorded. For example, if Matthew and Luke are merely chroniclers, how explain the different order they give for the Lord's temptations? Other differences will be mentioned in the course of this commentary. Historical criticism has saved us from a constant recourse to one theory after another to reconcile the discrepancies: accepting the priority of Mark, it is apparent that the other evangelists have sometimes *altered* Mark. The *second* view tries to have it both ways: that the Gospels (especially Mark, and perhaps the first draft of Luke, if it was written in two stages) both give us a reliable portrait of Jesus, and yet also have misunderstood or distorted (with dogmatic additions) the portrait they have so faithfully preserved. Elaborate attempts have been made to show that the very tenses in the Greek indicate unmistakable recollections on somebody's part of what is being described; yet the same observers, we are told, mistook the walking on the waters and the stilling of the storm. Exorcisms are proof of the authentic early tradition; but Jesus' cursing of the fig-tree (Mark 11.14) represents a popular local legend which has been foisted on to Jesus. It all seems to be self-contradictory. The *third* view involves complicated issues, but historical criticism does not necessarily lead to negative results. And history is important theologically: hence theologians, not least in Germany itself, have taken up again 'the quest of the historical Jesus',[1] since if the exalted Christ of the Church's faith be isolated from the humiliated Christ, the prophet of Nazareth, Christianity will degenerate into theosophy. If in Jesus

[1] See below, p. 23.

Christ we have an encounter with God, we must want to know more about this Jesus. Note for example the interest shown in the humanity of Jesus by the epistle to the Hebrews.

A fourth view about the Gospels is adopted in this commentary; a view which accepts the certainty of some literary relationship between the Gospels (viz. that Matthew and Luke used Mark), and welcomes the thesis of the Form Critics (such as Dr Bultmann) that the Gospels are written by believers for believers within the community of the Church, yet rejects their view that the evangelists were mere compilers who strung together without adequate connections the various stories that were circulating in the Church, just as it also rejects the extremely negative results of Form Criticism. Rather, each Gospel must be considered as a whole, as a literary unity with its own theological purpose. It was Fenton Hort (the Cambridge scholar who played a major part in getting out the Revised Version of the NT in 1881) who wrote to Bishop Lightfoot a hundred years ago, saying that though the evangelists are not three absolutely original writers, ' their independence of one another is most striking '. When they diverge it is of great interest to know why. It is suggested in this commentary that such divergences can be explained by understanding the evangelists' theology and the plans of their books. On this view of the Gospels, therefore, what they describe may have a deeper meaning than appears at first sight to the modern reader; and the evangelists are not merely rehabilitated as authors, but so also is the doctrine of inspiration, in that each evangelist has given the Church a creative and skilful construction of the words and deeds of Jesus in terms relevant to his own generation. Such a ' deeper meaning ' in the Gospels can be shown to be probable by considering the way in which the Bible as a whole treats numbers. Sometimes in the OT we are given discrepant figures in parallel narratives. Of course this can be explained in a superficial way by talking about sources and redactors, but the final redactor was no more stupid than we are and must have been aware of a discrepancy. Therefore, it is suggested, such figures may have a symbolical sense: they are designed to prove or confirm something. And when Joseph had his second dream (Genesis 37), he equated the twelve tribes of Israel with the twelve zodiacal constellations, and this had repercussions right down through the Bible as far as Rev. 12.1; 21.12. Another OT example is in Ex. 15.27. Turning to the NT, the number 666 of the Beast in Rev. 13.18 is widely agreed to have *some* symbolical significance, and probably this is also true of the 153 fishes of John 21.11. And there are many other numbers in the NT where one feels that the point is theological rather than merely arithmetical. Forty is a favourite, and it cannot be used in the NT without a wealth of OT background; seven, being the number of days of the week, has about it the idea of completeness; twelve too has rich OT associations, while three has acquired associations for the Church in view of Easter Day. It can hardly be an accident that of all the hundreds of healing miracles that he might have recounted, Mark actually restricted himself to twelve (plus one exceptional healing, of a Gentile), arranged not necessarily in chronological order, but in three groups, of five plus five plus two (so that the third of the second group is the raising of Jairus' daughter—it is also the eighth from the beginning, and for the Christian eight would recall the Sunday of the Resurrection); and these healings are integrated into the callings of the twelve apostles, among whom there is an inner group of three. (Luke has doubled Mark's healings: twenty-six people are healed, and they include a Samaritan and the servant of a Gentile centurion.)

This is but to say that the evangelists are Christian theologians who are writing an entirely new kind of literary

work, which they do with a clear purpose from a clear
standpoint. The meaning of their narrative is not confined to the literal and the historical: we are expected
to look more deeply, as indeed Mark in 8.14-21 himself
invites us to. Twelve healings indicate that Jesus did
historically confine his offer of salvation to the Jews. But
the thirteenth signifies the promise of the mission to the
Gentiles. It follows that each Gospel must be considered
as a whole and that we cannot satisfactorily dovetail
three or four Gospels together to form one continuous
narrative. Thus, it is impossible to harmonize all the
details in the resurrection narratives; it is difficult, and
undesirable, to combine the incidents in the Passion narratives in such a way as, for instance, to make an historical
sequence of the words from the cross. There is no doubt
at all about the historicity of the crucifixion, and it is
certain that Jesus uttered some last words. But what were
they? It is at first disappointing that Mark and Luke
record different words, but from the religious point of
view this is not really a disadvantage. Neither Mark nor
Luke is a pedestrian chronicler, and they interpret, for
use in apologetic, instruction and worship, the tradition
which they have received. Listening to them, we are listening to what the exalted Lord of the Church, who was no
dead figure of the past, was himself saying to successive
generations of practising Christians.

In his commentary on the Fourth Gospel Bishop Westcott said: ' The conditions of the historian's work include
in every case choice, compression, combination of materials. And he fulfils his work rightly who chooses, compres-
ses and combines his materials according to a certain
vital proportion. In other words, the historian, like the
poet, cannot but interpret the facts which he records. The
truth of history is simply the truth of the interpretation
of an infinitude of details contemplated together. The
simplest statement of a result presents a broad generaliza-

tion of particulars . . . and represents a total impression
of the particulars seen in one way. It does not represent
either all the particulars or all the impressions which they
are capable of producing. What is called pure "objec-
tive" history is a mere phantom. No one could specify . . .
all the separate details which man's most imperfect observation can distinguish as elements in any one "fact";
and the least reflection shows that there are other elements
not less numerous or less important than those open to
our observation which cannot be observed by us and
which yet go to the fulness of the "fact". The subjectivity
of history is consequently a mere question of degree.'
And when the 'fact' is Jesus Christ then everything
could never be entirely said by one or three or four people;
the whole Christ cannot be wholly described; he cannot
be exhausted in terms of perception. There was a complex situation which the evangelists invite us to decide about,
a complex situation which included the impression made by
Jesus on the Church which produced the Gospels. For
what the fourth evangelist said of his book, 'These things
are written that ye may believe that Jesus is the Christ'
is equally true of the synoptists; and what a modern
commentator says of the Fourth Gospel can equally be
applied to Luke: 'He sought to draw out, using in part
the form and style of narrative (and that he did use this
form is itself highly significant), the true meaning of the
life and death of one whom he believed to be the Son
of God, a being from beyond history' (C. K. Barrett, *The
Gospel according to St John*, 1955, p. 117).

St Luke's task was governed by the delay in the return
of Christ which at first had been expected very soon. He
had to interpret for a puzzled Church the words of Jesus
about eschatology and to give answers to the kind of
question mentioned in Acts 1.6. He had too to consider
how Jesus manifested himself in the era between the
Resurrection and the Second Coming and what was the

theological significance of the unexpectedly extended era
of the Church. Luke's answer is to show that the sacred
history is composed of three layers. (1) The history of
Israel; (2) the history of Jesus, the mid-point of the whole;
and (3) the history of the Church, which is the continuation
of the work of Jesus. The second is the fulfilment of the
first, and the third is the continuation into a prolonged future of the second. Luke sets about showing this in the way he writes his Gospel and the Acts.
Though he does not do it so clearly as Matthew does,
Luke writes his Gospel to correspond to the first six
books of the OT. He had his new Genesis, which describes
the birth and infancy of Jesus, the beginning of the New
Creation; there is the new Exodus, with the temptations
for forty days in the wilderness; there is Leviticus, with
the institution and charge of the Twelve and 'the ordina-
tion sermon of the new Levites' (Farrer), 6.20 ff. The
new Numbers gives us the mission of the Seventy. But the
longest section of all is Luke's new Deuteronomy in which
he collects numerous pieces of teaching from Matthew
and Mark and in 9.51-18.14 sets them out deliberately
in an order to follow that of the OT Deuteronomy. It
is Luke's way of showing that Jesus is the 'prophet like
unto Moses' whose coming was predicted in Deut. 18.15,
18 and that Christ is the true Mediator between God and
man, having superseded the Jewish Law (Torah) in this
rôle. Luke's Book of Joshua (Hebrew form of 'Jesus')
is obviously the Passion and Resurrection narratives:
repentant Rahab of Jericho is paralleled by the repentant
Zacchaeus (19.1, 2) and the incident can be assigned to
Jericho because Luke has made the healing of the blind
man (18.35 ff.) *precede* Jesus' entry into the city. Cf. Mark
10.46. The details of this arrangement may be studied in
the essays by Prof. C. F. Evans and Dr A. M. Farrer in
Studies in the Gospels (edited by D. E. Nineham, 1955),
but it should be remembered that the artificial Hexateuchal

schemes of the Gospels only make explicit what our Lord himself actually was. He *was* the mediator of a new covenant, and was not merely imagined to be so by a theologian's prolonged reflection. He was himself 'the one who compelled his followers to think out the meaning of what he had done and said, in terms which had once been applicable to Moses and the Torah, but which must for ever afterwards be appropriate only to him' (Alan Richardson, *An Introduction to the Theology of the New Testament*, 1958, p. 168).

Now this theory of the composition of Luke has certain implications. It means that Luke was an able theologian who, writing more of the NT than any other single author, wrote it, like a poem, as a unity, and from the Church's standpoint. For this view gives more substance to the 'inspiration' of the evangelists than the process of composition that is more usually held. According to this more usual view, there existed in the early Church alongside the Gospel of Mark a collection of Jesus' sayings with some narrative, but excluding the Passion story, written in Greek and which has never been found as a separate document, but, it is inferred, was known to the authors of Matthew and Luke. Their having both used this lost document accounts for their having so much material in common, over and above their common Marcan material (for they also both used Mark). Since the time when Dr Armitage Robinson used to lecture at Cambridge, before 1900, the symbol Q has been generally employed for this hypothetical source.[1] It has been further held that the third Gospel was written in distinct stages, which can be traced: first Luke combined Q with a number of stories about Jesus and parables which were circulating in his own church, and then at a later date (perhaps

[1] There is also evidence that this symbol was already being used in Germany by Bernhard Weiss, and that he had borrowed it from his father.

even after writing Acts) he stumbled across Mark and decided to combine his first version of the Gospel ('Proto-Luke') with his new discovery; while later still he added the infancy narratives. By contrast, the theory advocated here is that the third Gospel was conceived as a unity. The author used Mark as his basis (he reproduces more than half Mark's 661 verses), and he also knew Matthew, where indeed he found a Gospel written to a pattern corresponding to the first six books of the OT. Luke picked out what he required from Matthew as he needed it for his own plan, and sometimes (e.g. at 8.25) he deliberately follows Matthew (8.27) rather than Mark (4.41). So there never was a 'lost document'—though, provided that we are not implying a theory about the composition of the Gospels, there is no reason why we should not go on using the symbol Q to describe the material which Matthew and Luke share in common.

The arguments for dispensing with the Q hypothesis have been stated at length by Dr Farrer, but long ago there were hints of dissatisfaction with it in the books of Dr R. H. Lightfoot and Dr J. H. Ropes. The latter said that 'the grounds on which Q's existence is inferred by modern scholars are far less secure than is commonly represented or supposed'. Briefly, one objection to the hypothesis of a lost document is the improbability of any early Christian work about Jesus being written which stopped short of the crucifixion, and yet the agreements of words and order between Matthew and Luke are often so close that it is hard to think they both had access to a body of tradition that was being passed on orally. The view that Luke knew Matthew—though admittedly rejected by most of the experts—does account both for the large area of agreement between Matthew and Luke in non-Marcan material, and also for the cases in material common to all three synoptists where Luke has chosen to follow Matthew in preference to Mark.

ESCHATOLOGY

Luke's particular contribution to the theology of the
Church was to interpret Jesus' eschatological teaching for
the generation after the fall of Jerusalem (AD 70), when
the Temple had been destroyed, the Jewish-Christian community had fled, and (by the time that Luke was writing,
ten years or so later), the centre of authority in the Church
had moved to the Gentile world and that Church was still
expanding. Now the Jews had expected that one day in the
future God would close down the present world order;
though when and how were matters of dispute. The Last
Events (hence the word *eschatology*) would disclose the
meaning of all preceding historical events, by showing what
they had led to. The startling message of Jesus was that
these Last Events were being set in train by himself, and
that men were indeed seeing some of the things that past
history was leading up to. His works of power such as
the exorcisms and his teaching 'with authority' were signs
of what was going on, if only people would realize it.
Jesus' Passion, Death and Resurrection were themselves
the very events by which the Kingdom, or rule, or kingship, of God was present in the world. The obedience of
Jesus was the triumph of God.

There are however sayings of Jesus recorded in the
synoptic Gospels which assert that the Kingdom of God
will not be completely there until Jesus returns again, and
there are many references throughout the NT to this future
'Parousia' of Jesus. There have been periods in the life
of the Christian Church when these sayings were almost
forgotten and it was Dr Albert Schweitzer's book *The
Quest of the Historical Jesus* (ET. 1910; 3rd ed., 1954) that
convinced students that the eschatological sayings were a
very important element in the authentic teaching of Jesus.
But since he did not return, was Jesus then after all (as
Schweitzer himself concluded) just a deluded visionary?

For half a century and more Christian theologians have
been considering the problem posed by *The Quest*. Several
energetic attempts have been made to show that St Paul
and other writers of the NT misunderstood what our Lord
had in fact taught and that he did not predict any future
coming again. But it always remains puzzling why, if this
is so, the Church should have embarrassed itself by so soon
making this addition to its creed. In one of his earliest epistles
(I Thessalonians) St Paul had to go into some ' very elaborate,
rather obscure and not immediately convincing details about
a future historical occurrence ' (E. L. Mascall), and as late as
the time of II Peter (3.4) there were Christians in despair:
'Where is the promise of his coming? '

It is likely therefore that our Lord said that he would
return again, and that this would be the signal for the Last
Judgement, and the end of the world; and that his coming
would be sudden and unexpected. ' Whosoever shall be
ashamed of me and of my words in this adulterous and
sinful generation, the Son of man also shall be ashamed
of him, when he cometh in the glory of his Father with
the holy angels' (Mark 8.38). Under the sense of the
terrible responsibility of right personal decision and of
the urgency of the Church's task to be accomplished, the
suddenness of the Lord's Parousia was expressed in the
Church under the form of an *imminent* return, and the
inevitable reaction of disappointment and disillusion is
the background to Luke-Acts.

Luke wrote to show that the death, resurrection and
exaltation of Jesus were not intended to be immediately
followed by the Parousia—not even after the fall of Jerusalem which Jesus had predicted. The providential delay
should be the cause of thankfulness, since they had the
presence of the Spirit: even though they had to ' wait for
a Saviour', they possessed a ' citizenship in heaven'
(Phil. 3.20). Christ did come, and come repeatedly, to his
disciples, though not in apocalyptic splendour. Luke thus

gives a positive theological content to the period of delay, and he does it not by re-writing the gospel tradition (as John was to do), but by making adjustments to the material he already had. Thus, in case Mark 14.62 should be mis-understood as a reference to an immediate return of the Lord, Luke omits the words 'Ye shall see' and 'coming', so that his 22.69 reads, 'from henceforth shall the Son of man be seated at the right hand of the power of God', which unmistakably confines the reference to the Ascension. Similarly Luke adjusts Mark 9.1 for his own generation. Mark had read, 'There be some . . . which shall in no wise taste of death, till they see the kingdom of God come with power'. Luke 9.27 omits the last three words.

Luke therefore shows that according to the teaching of Jesus there is a 'kingdom' of the Messiah, lasting over the period between the Resurrection and the Parousia which will usher in the Kingdom of God in its fulness. According to S. Mowinckel, *He that cometh*, ET 1956, p. 321, and other authorities, the rabbis already conceived of an interim kingdom before the final Kingdom of glory under the kingly rule of God, and so Jesus has adopted a Jewish conception. Matt. 25.34 seems to be further evidence that this was Jesus' teaching. Therefore, by Christ's acts of redemption we have been admitted to his Kingdom (Col. 1.12-14), and in due course we may enter the kingdom of God in its fulness, the kingdom which flesh and blood cannot enter (I Cor. 15.50). The apostles have Christ's authority (Matt. 28.18-20); and are entrusted with a kingdom (Luke 22.29); the Church has received his Spirit (Acts) and is destined to have a work to do until the Parousia, after which God the Father shall be 'all in all' (I Cor. 15.28).

There was a time in the nineteen-thirties when Luke was out of favour. Mark had been rediscovered as a powerful book, portraying an awesome, mysterious figure, always under the shadow of the Cross and who remains 'for the most part hidden from us', while Luke by contrast seemed to give us a Jesus who was more human than divine; whom we could love for his gentleness and imitate in his prayerfulness, but hardly worship! Luke's two-volume work appeared to come much nearer to the secular type of biography. There has however now been time to reconsider this verdict. Luke is in fact a theologian who grappled with the problem that has worried us: whether Jesus' sayings about his second coming discredit the saving message. Luke's answer can be ours: that Christ reconstituted the People of God, who are now the Church of Christ, the Kingdom of Christ (Acts 20.25), whose marks are repentance towards God and faith towards Christ (Acts 20.21), and by baptism we are admitted into the Body which cannot be separated from Christ. Christ works through the Church universally as once in the days of his flesh he did locally. The Church's works are his works: and so the healings in Acts are written to parallel the healings in the third Gospel: 'as Jesus fulfilled the prophecy of Isa. 35.6 by making the lame to walk, so Peter and John fulfil it even more literally. . . . St Peter's cure of Aeneas recalls . . . the healing of the paralytic by Jesus, and the raising of Dorcas . . . that of Jairus' daughter' (G. W. H. Lampe, who gives further parallels in his essay in *Studies in the Gospels*, ed. D. E. Nineham). So the glory and the victory that Mark concentrates into the Cross and a hint of Resurrection are spread out by Luke *back* into Jesus' infancy and ministry and *forward* into the Church. Simeon sees the glory of Israel (2.32); *words of grace* were heard at Nazareth (4.22); the rending of the Temple veil which follows, and *emphasises*, Jesus' death in Mark precedes it in Luke. In the Acts persecution of the Church is equivalent to persecuting Jesus (Acts 9.4), for the Church is the place of his presence. Jesus is not just an historical figure of the past (3.1); his power works within the Christian community which accepts him as Lord. So he lives today.

THE ETHICAL TEACHING OF JESUS

In the Bible ethics are always related to a set of convictions about what God has done; and the kind of law promulgated depends on the kind of gospel proclaimed. In the epistles, Gospel and Law are sometimes interspersed, as in Hebrews, while sometimes, as with Romans, a first part deals with various religious themes in a reflective and theological manner, while a second part consists of precepts and admonitions. In the Gospels, narrative about the works of the Messiah is combined with specimens of his teaching. For example, in Matthew one collection of teaching material is given after the Lord's baptism in the Jordan and his forty days' trial in the wilderness, and answers to the Old Law given by Moses after Israel's 'baptism' (I Cor. 10.2) and trials in the wilderness.

In Matthew the Lord, as the New Moses, delivers his New Law on the mountain. In Luke the Sermon, with some variations, is delivered explicitly on the level ground, presumably so that Jesus' coming down to it may foreshadow his descent from heaven to judge the nations at the end of the world. But notwithstanding these differences of context, the interpretation of both sermons (on the Mount and on the Plain) must proceed along the same lines. These lines have differed enormously however amongst readers of the Gospels. Nietzsche, as an unbeliever, regarded the New Law as a catalogue of precepts which 'paltry people have stuffed into their heads' and he cannot read the Gospels without a feeling of preference for everything in them which is the object of condemnation. Renan on the other hand conceded that the ethical teaching of Jesus 'will never be surpassed', while in his life of Voltaire (1872, p. 179), Lord Morley writes: 'It cannot be too often repeated that the Christianity which Voltaire assailed was not that of the Sermon on the Mount, for there was not a man then alive more keenly sensible than he was of the generous humanity which is there enjoined with a force that so strangely touches the heart, nor one who was on the whole, in spite of constitutional infirmities and words which were far worse than his deeds, more ardent and persevering in its practice.'

Christian believers on the other hand have been no less divided about the interpretation of the Sermon. Most commentators have taken the view that the Lord's injunctions are precepts which can be put into practice, at any rate with the help of grace, though not always literally, for Jesus was not legislating so much as indicating, with all sorts of picturesque oriental hyperboles, the kind of direction that Christian conduct should take. On the other hand, there is a tradition in Reformed theology which regards the Lord's teaching as statements of an impossible ideal: whereas the Jews had their law, which a good man might strive to observe in full, Christ's demand, which is for perfection, could never be observed by sinful men. That is why his particular precepts seem to take the form of extravagant demands whose practice would be irreconcilable with living in the world at all, such as the command to ' hate' one's relatives (Luke 14.26) or not to offer resistance (even non-violent resistance) to evil (Matt. 5.39). On this (Reformed) interpretation, the ethical teaching has a double significance. It states the ideal to which Christians must try to approximate; but because they fall short they are made aware of their sinful state and their helplessness except Christ save them. This is a pessimistic view of the possibilities of sanctity, but it does take seriously the NT eschatology that the Kingdom of God has not yet fully come, so that of course there cannot yet be any perfection. But does it take equally seriously the assertions that the Kingdom of *Christ* is present and that his Spirit is at work in the Church? The ethical teaching must surely be related to this double character of the eschatology, in the following way. Some of our Lord's commands can, with his help, be put into practice; others are attempts to state the absolute law of love (which will prevail in the perfect Kingdom of God) in terms of this-worldly situations, and so of course they have the character of paradox. Putting it another way: in the Kingdom of God we shall be perfect in that mode of being called the Resurrection Body; but meanwhile, in this present life, we are called upon to translate perfect love into the complicated and complex situations of daily life. In the transcendent Kingdom there will exist a community of perfect love, in which there will be no enemies to be loved or beggars to be fed; but since this absolute love does not exist before the Parousia, the concrete instances which Jesus gives of what embracing the Kingdom may involve are bound to be expressed in 'hard sayings' like Matt. 5.41.

Take an example. Jesus tells us, simply, that we are not to be anxious. Yet anxiety is, as Paul Tillich remarked, 'the permanent whisper in the depth of our being'. We cannot escape from it. Jesus therefore means: in the Kingdom of God his peace will totally exclude anxiety; but in this era in which the struggle against evil goes on the promise can only be presented as a command, to trust. By repeated acts of trust we learn, from the circumference as it were, of the peace of God's Kingdom.

The Christian life is both a possession and an expectation. We are already risen with Christ (Col. 3.1), but it is not yet made manifest what we shall be (I John 3.2). We do even now enjoy a foretaste of the joy and love which in their fulness will be proper to the Kingdom of God.

THE MIRACLES OF JESUS

The importance which miracles have in the Bible as a whole is undeniable, and they are distinguished both in character and purpose from the prodigies described in pagan writers (as when a man is turned into an animal) and from the magical displays of contemporary thaumaturges, all of which are incompatible with Jewish and Christian conceptions of a God who created the world and who retains his sovereignty over it. Hence the accusation rejected in Luke 11.15, the refusal of any sign but that of the prophet Jonah (11.29), and Jesus' silence before the curiosity of Herod (23.8-9). Miracles in the Bible are related to God's saving purposes for mankind; they are dynamic acts of the divine initiative against the disorder of a fallen universe. In the Gospels the miracles of Jesus are regarded as signs of the dawning of the Messianic era and are selected by the evangelists with skill and related with delicacy and restraint in order to make this quite clear. John's Gospel contains only seven miracles, so told as to be signs—indeed that is the word he employs—of the restorative power of God at work.

The healing miracles of the Gospels are not told because they are marvellous, or even because they are unique: for it is agreed that the Pharisees could also work exorcisms (Luke 11.19). They are 'miracles' in that they fulfil OT expectations, but they are not necessarily breaches of the laws of nature, and could have been wrought by a mechanism within Jesus' human nature which is explicable by modern psychological science, or by other forces latent in Nature which we have not yet discovered. The healings and exorcisms are therefore miraculous in virtue of their place and function in the story of the people of God; and they are certainly signs also of God's intervention inasmuch as they are natural forces set in motion in response to prayer (Mark 7.34). They can be called miracles of the first level, and their physical benefits are connected with the righteousness of God and the forgiveness of the sinner.

On the other hand there are miracles described in the Gospels which are undoubtedly disturbances of the natural order as known by us, such as Jesus' walking on the water, the multiplication of the loaves, the raising of the dead, and, one might add, the healings at a distance: these are

miracles of the second level. They too have a rôle as
signs of the Messianic era: they fulfil the anticipations of
the OT and point forward to the Kingdom of God. Moreover, similar stories told of pagan heroes, though by
comparison with the NT miracles they seem wholly
fantastic and arbitrary, yet are evidence that deep in the
soul of humanity was a conviction that these things ought
to be. In Christ their fantasies become historical facts:
the cosmological miracles of the Gospels signify the end
of humanity's yearnings; they speak of the unmerited grace
of God; of a love which is both mysterious and overwhelm-
ing, evoking a faith in Jesus who brings the Kingdom
of God. The view taken in this commentary is that
such miracles are not to be rejected, as though the
sovereign Creator God was unable to mould the material
he had made into special conformity with his intention.
As Dr Farrer has written, criticizing Dr Bultmann: 'Bultmann writes as though . . . the Word never becomes flesh
by making physical fact as immediately pliable to his
expression as spoken symbols are. Bultmann seems to be
convinced that he knows this, but I am not convinced that
I know it, and I cannot be made to agree by the authority
of the truism that symbolism ought not to be taken for
physical fact. For it still ought to be taken for physical
fact, if and where God has made it into physical fact'
(in *Kerygma and Myth*, ed. H. W. Bartsch, ET, 1953, p.
216). (For further reading: John Locke, *A Discourse of
Miracles*, ed. I. T. Ramsey, 1958; A. Richardson, *The
Miracle Stories of the Gospels*, 1952; C. S. Lewis, *Miracles*,
1952; *The Miracles and the Resurrection*, S.P.C.K. Theological Collection, No. 3, 1964; and C. F. D. Moule, ed.,
Miracles, 1965.)

AUTHORSHIP OF THE GOSPEL

Our opinion about who wrote the third Gospel will
depend on what we think of the authorship of the Acts, for

obviously they come from the same hand. The traditional view that Luke-Acts was written by 'Luke, the beloved physician' (Col. 4.14), who has incorporated part of his own diary, the travel narrative, in the Acts, has difficulties on account of some apparent discrepancies with the epistle to the Galatians; but these can be resolved (see W. L. Knox, *The Acts of the Apostles*, 1948) and there is some internal evidence to support the unanimous external evidence (i.e. the references in the early Fathers). For example, while technical medical terms did not exist in the ancient world and therefore nothing can be proved by any so-called medical vocabulary in Luke-Acts, it is surely significant that the third Gospel (8.43) in re-telling the story of the woman with an issue of blood omits from Mark 5.26 the note that her long medical treatment had only made her worse!

This question of authorship is discussed in the introduction to Dr R. R. Williams' commentary on the Acts in this series. He decides in favour of Lucan authorship as 'the most probable hypothesis', and inclines to an early date for both volumes. The view taken here about the date of composition is that Luke knows both Mark and Matthew and that Luke 21.20 has amended Mark 13.14 in the light of the historical experience of the fall of Jerusalem in AD 70. This is more likely than the views that the words are an instance of paranormal precognition or a natural recollection of past precedents. Of course Jerusalem had been 'compassed with armies' in OT times, as when Nebuchadnezzar laid siege to the city in 586 BC; but the fact that Luke has made this alteration to Mark suggests that he knows of a recent event which obliges him to write so. In this case Luke was written between 80-90; a date earlier than 80 is unlikely, for the reason mentioned in the commentary at 6.15.

BIBLIOGRAPHY

COMMENTARIES

G. B. Caird, 271 pp., 1963
E. E. Ellis, 300 pp., 1966
A. R. C. Leaney, 300 pp., 1958

OTHER WORKS

HANS CONZELMANN, *The Theology of Saint Luke*, 255 pp., 1960

AUSTIN FARRER, *St Matthew and St Mark*, 238 pp., 2nd ed. 1966

M. D. GOULDER, *Type and History in Acts*, 252 pp., 1964

J. JEREMIAS, *New Testament Theology*, I, 330 pp., 1971

G. W. H. LAMPE and K. J. WOOLLCOMBE, *Essays on Typology*, 80 pp., 1957

H. K. MCARTHUR, *In Search of the Historical Jesus*, 284 pp., 1970

C. F. D. MOULE, *The Birth of the New Testament*, 252 pp., 2nd ed. 1966

D. E. NINEHAM (ed.), *Studies in the Gospels*, 262 pp., 1955

J. ROHDE, *Rediscovering the Teaching of the Evangelists*, 278 pp., 1968

J. H. ROPES, *The Synoptic Gospels*, 117 pp., 2nd ed. 1960

E. SCHWEIZER, *Jesus*, 200 pp., 1971

The Commentary is based upon the Revised Version of 1881 (RV). Reference is sometimes made to its margins (RV marg.), to the Revised Standard Version (RSV), to the Authorized, or King James, Version (AV), and to the New English Bible (NEB). ET indicates an English translation. OT stands for Old Testament; NT for New Testament.

COMMENTARY

I & II

THE PREFACE

1.1-4

The author acknowledges the existence of predecessors (perhaps Mark and Matthew) who have inspired him to undertake a similar task, and the help of eye-witnesses. It is the latter who have delivered THE WORD, the whole course of sacred events 'most surely believed among us' (AV), and who are probably to be identified with the Twelve who 'went in and went out among us, beginning from the baptism of John' (Acts 1.21 f.). Any other eye-witnesses were poor inhabitants of Palestine who did not travel like St Paul, and who were unknown in the Gentile churches, though of course Luke may have sought them out if he was at Caesarea with St Paul. If these verses were intended as the preface to the whole work ('Luke-Acts'), then EYE-WITNESSES might possibly extend to some of the Gentile Christians of St Paul's churches which Luke did not himself visit. The dedication to THEOPHILUS, a distinguished citizen (of Antioch?) either baptized or under instruction, does not imply that the book was intended only for private use. Indeed exactly the opposite: and it has even been held that the name Theophilus (='Friend of God') was no more than a literary device for a preface which was imitating contemporary writings with the aim of securing a wide circulation.

The whole work divides roughly into two equal parts (Gospel and Acts). Though some NT authors may have written their manuscript in the new book, or codex, form, it is possible that Luke happened to prefer the old rolls of papyrus, and if so the Gospel would have needed about 31 feet.

THE INFANCY NARRATIVE

1.5-2. end

The sudden transition from a piece of Greek that would not have shamed Thucydides to the Hebrew style and atmosphere of the infancy narrative is abrupt and it has sometimes been suggested that Luke made use of a Hebrew or Aramaic document which he has translated rather literally into Greek. Nor was Marcion (anti-Jewish heretic of the second century) the last to hold that these chapters are from another hand altogether. The style was however analysed by Harnack and by H. J. Cadbury, who both wrote with the authority which comes from many years' study of the Lucan writings, and they concluded that the unmistakable variation of style in the first two chapters can be accounted for on the assumption that the author inevitably reproduced the language of the Greek OT when his thoughts were so much occupied with the OT background of the events described. This opinion has not satisfied everybody, but it is confirmed by the plan of the Gospel, which does seem to argue a single author for the whole. Persons and notions of chs. 1-2 anticipate what is to come in 3-24, as with the Baptist and the prophecy of Simeon. Theological ideas in 1-2 about the importance of Jerusalem, the blessedness of poverty, the rôle of the Spirit at moments of Messianic significance, are developed later in the Gospel.

But if the first two chapters are an integral part of the Gospel, they admittedly stand somewhat apart from the subsequent chapters in as much as they fall into that character of Jewish literature known as *midrash*, which consisted of reflections upon the sacred text designed to clarify the theological meaning of certain basic historical events. Such reflections did not necessarily comprise historical fictions—though many did—and it was a natural means for both Matthew and Luke to impart their instruction about the unique Christ-events. Each of their stories has its own precise purpose and it must be confessed that this is easier to discover than it is to demonstrate the positive historical content. Nevertheless the label *midrash* is not a device for avoiding these awkward questions of historicity or for denying the traditional view that chs 1-2 embody some authentic reminiscences of Mary. But knowing the sort of literary *genre* that they belong to, we should not first of all examine them to see if they are history or legend. Rather, we shall ask first what the language of the evangelist is straining to disclose. What attitudes and responses does he seek to win from his readers? We shall then, secondly, be grateful for the historical information they happen to contain, which, in the view of this commentary, would include the fact of Jesus' birth without a human father, the persons and names of Jesus, Mary and Joseph, the obscurity of the home at Nazareth, and the family visits to Jerusalem.

The very arrangement of the material brings out the theological message. The birth of the Baptist and the birth of Jesus are carefully related so that the pattern of the first is followed, with significant variations, by the second. The birth, circumcision and manifestation of John, who GREW, AND WAXED STRONG IN SPIRIT (1.80) is followed by the account of the birth, circumcision and manifestation of Jesus, who GREW, AND WAXED STRONG (2.40). And there are many other parallels in the two stories: but to what end? Luke's intention is to point the contrast between John and Jesus: thus, Zacharias shows a reprehensible lack of faith —by contrast with Mary: John will be great *before God*— but Jesus will be great without qualification (in the psalms *God* is called great): John's mission is that of preparation

—Jesus has an eternal mission. And this divine status of Jesus is frequently indicated by Luke by the use of language derived from the OT, notably the books of Daniel (chs 9-10) and Malachi (chs 3-4). In Daniel it is Gabriel (mentioned twice) who predicts that there are seventy weeks until the coming of 'everlasting righteousness', while in the Gospel it is again Gabriel (mentioned twice) who announces, in effect, that the Messianic age has dawned. (From the announcement to Zacharias to the presentation in the Temple is 490 days, i.e. 70 weeks.) Luke 1.16 f., 76, seem to derive entirely from the verses in Malachi 3-4 in which Yahweh's 'messenger' is to prepare his way and turn the hearts of the fathers to the children. This messenger (cf. Luke 7.27) is identified with the Baptist. Now Malachi's messenger is to prepare the way for God: the Baptist is to prepare the way for Jesus. And in Mal. 3.1, the Lord is to come suddenly to his temple; in Luke 2.22-39 Jesus comes there. Both passages are eschatological, in the sense that for Luke the time of fulfilment which the prophets spoke of as the 'last age' has now arrived. The Glory of the Lord which 'filled the tabernacle' in Ex. 40.35, is seen by the eyes of Simeon (Luke 2.32) inside the Temple. It is a tremendous moment in the history of revelation and Luke has made use of OT concepts (as of course he naturally would; ever since he had been a proselyte the OT had been his library) to make his meaning perfectly plain. The pity of it is that what is so clear in Luke was obscured by the liturgies which call the event, 'The Purification of St Mary the Virgin'.

This explains an interesting difference between Luke and the other two synoptists. For Matthew and Mark Jesus fulfilled the Malachi prophecy in Holy Week when he at last came up to Jerusalem and proceeded to cleanse the Temple. Because Luke has put the fulfilment of Malachi at the Presentation (ch. 2) he does record the bare fact of the cleansing of the Temple, but the account is very much abbreviated (19.45, 46) and it does not occupy the strategic theological location that it has in Mark.

.   .   .   .

Zacharias' behaviour recalls that of Abraham when he ('well-stricken in age') was told that his wife, hitherto barren, was to bear a son. WHEREBY SHALL I KNOW THIS? (18), he demurs, just as Abraham also hesitated (Gen. 15.8). Luke is presenting his account as being the opening stage of the history of the New Israel (as St Paul regards the Christian People, Gal. 6.16), and therefore this section is designed to correspond to the historical beginnings of old Israel.

13. John

In Hebrew there would be a play upon words between THY SUPPLICATION IS HEARD and JOHN. BECAUSE the supplication is heard, *therefore* he is to be called John. (Cf. Gen. 5.29 etc.) This is evidence that this story could not have been first composed in Greek. It could be a piece of authentic reminiscence. In 7.28 it is explained that John marks the end of the OT era, and (it has been suggested) this is also indicated here in the infancy narrative. For in the OT the book which comes before Malachi is Zechariah, a fact which may well have suggested the name for John's father. And it so happens that another Zechariah was the last of the OT martyrs; he was also a priest (II Chron. 24.20) who served in the Temple. In this case the name Zacharias is probably not an historical reminiscence but is devised by Luke to indicate that John is the culmination of all the OT prophets and the last martyr of the old Israel; henceforward, Luke means, the new order is in operation, with its apostles and prophets and, his readers knew, Christian martyrs.

14-15.
Gabriel's address recalls the words of the angel to Manoah's wife when the birth of Samson was promised. And Samson was the *last* of the judges—yet another indic-

ation of Luke's theme that the old dispensation is over and is now being fulfilled in Jesus Christ and his Church.

19. to bring . . . good tidings

One word in the Greek (*euangelizesthai*); it is a common verb in Luke-Acts and in the epistles of St Paul and is usually translated 'to preach the gospel'. Certainly the angel is here referring to gospel events, concerning our salvation.

20. thou shalt be silent

Like Daniel (Dan. 10.15), Zacharias became dumb. Nevertheless he continued his priestly duties in the Temple until the end of his term. After this scene, Elizabeth conceives her child. There is no hint of a *virgin* birth.

26 ff. *The Annunciation*

The promise to Mary reproduces that to Elizabeth, but to Zacharias' hesitation corresponds—Mary's obedience. The words of Gabriel derive from Isaiah, where, in 7.14, the prophet had given a sign that a certain *young woman* should bring forth a child and that before he reaches the age of discernment (7.16) the danger to the nation will be over. Luke (who knows the OT in the Greek version, where *parthenos*, which usually means *virgin*, is the noun chosen) at any rate takes the word to mean *virgin* and with a clear reference to Isa. 9.6-7, Jesus is shown to be at once a supernatural being and a descendant of the house of David.

27. Mary and Joseph are engaged, but have not had sexual intercourse.

35. overshadow

The meaning can only be grasped by recalling the 'cloud' which 'covered' the tent of meeting in the book of Exodus, when the Lord's glory filled the tabernacle. Here it is Mary who is filled with the glory which was Jesus. The cloud was a conventional symbol to denote the presence of God; and so we shall find that at the Transfiguration a cloud will cover Jesus and the three disciples and at the Ascension a cloud will conceal him from the disciples. Such was the kind of language which a Jew was bound to employ when he would describe the birth of the Son of God.

39-45. The Visitation

Mary, now pregnant, goes to the house of Zacharias for ABOUT THREE MONTHS (56). Luke's words echo the story of II Samuel 6 where David takes the ark (in which according to Hebrew thought, Num. 10.35, was the very presence of God) to the house of Obed-Edom for three months while on the way to Jerusalem. The OT narrative is an account, in an historical form, of the festival which was held to mark the installation of David as king in Jerusalem. Similarly, Mary carries the Christ, and the narrative will bring them soon to Jerusalem; and just as then the crowds rejoiced and David leaped, now Elizabeth rejoices and the babe leaps in the womb. True, the word used in the Greek for LEAPED is not the same as that in II Sam. 6.16, but this may be because Luke 1-2 as a new Genesis also has in mind the quickening in Rebekah's womb recorded in Gen. 25.22, where the Greek verb is the same as that in Luke 1.41.

46-55. The Magnificat

Readers of the Gospel have often remarked the resemblance of the Magnificat to the thanksgiving of Hannah for the birth of Samuel (I Samuel 2). Now this used to be interpreted by Jews of the first century as a song of Israel. Perhaps Luke is therefore regarding Mary as the mouthpiece of Israel: through her the Chosen People makes thanksgiving; Mary is the fulfilment of all the prophecies about the virgin daughter of Sion who is in travail (Micah and Jeremiah) but who is to *rejoice* (Zeph. 3.14; cf. Luke 1.28—same Greek word). It is not surprising that the RV margin notices so many reminiscences of the psalms of David; the words of King David are appropriate enough in the mouth of the mother of Israel's new King. (But the RV margin should also have compared the last words of the Magnificat with the last words of David's song in II Sam. 22.) God has looked on the humiliation of Mary (who is Sion); and now she is exalted. Therefore shall all the generations to come call her blessed (Mary, but also the Chosen People, soon to be the Body of Christ); for in her (Mary; but also the Church, which is the Temple of God, I Cor, 3.16 f.; cf. Rev. 15.8) dwelt the glory of God. As the Virgin Mother brings forth the Word of God, the Church brings forth that Word—for all mankind.

59. they would have called him . . . after the name of his father

There is no other evidence for the Jewish custom of giving the name at the time of circumcision. But Luke is not likely to have made a mistake; and the custom is known among other peoples who practised the rite.

62. they made signs

So it would seem that Zacharias had been rendered deaf as well as dumb. The tablet was of wood, and either it was covered with parchment or it had a hollow surface into which wax had been poured.

67-79. *The Benedictus*

The Song of Zacharias, like the Magnificat, is a thanksgiving for the approaching salvation, and no more than two verses (76-77) explicitly allude to John; thus his subordinate rôle is made plain. He will precede THE LORD. The canticle may have been a Jewish song in existence before this Gospel was written; in which case the ENEMIES would have been the Romans and the hymn an expression of longing for deliverance and for the coming of *the Messiah* who would, in Jewish expectation, prepare the way of the Lord, i.e. God. But Luke at any rate intends us to understand THE LORD of 76 to be Jesus (cf. THE MOTHER OF MY LORD, 43), while the ENEMIES are the hostile powers who encompass the believer and oppose the Word.

69. a horn
A symbol of strength, as in I Sam. 2.10.

77. the remission of their sins
This is the kind of salvation that Jesus would bring. It would not be political liberation.

78. the dayspring from on high
God will come and help us; presumably derived from Mal. 4.2 which speaks of the sun of righteousness (how lucky English is to be able to make the pun) arising with healing in his wings. The early Church often referred to Christ's resurrection under the metaphor of the rising sun, and the first day of the week is indeed appropriately named. But the symbolism associated with Hellenistic sun-worship which the Church boldy took over was uncompromisingly referred to the historical Person of her founder (H. Rahner, *Greek Myths and Christian Mystery*, 1963).

79. the way of peace
As often in the OT, a Messianic promise is accompanied by the expectation of peace. Isaiah said that the Messiah would be a Prince of Peace. In the Gospel peace will again be proclaimed by the angels and by Simeon; while in the Acts (10.36) the apostle will preach the gospel of peace by Jesus Christ who 'is Lord of all'. Fundamentally this peace denotes reconciliation—of God to men, and of men to each other. But the NT does not unambiguously specify any particular attitude to *international war* and peace. War and conflicts are to be expected to the end of time owing to human sin: nevertheless because Christ has manifested

his sovereignty over sin and death, the Church must constantly question decisions of statesmen which are taken without any reference to morality. Bishop George Bell, and others, courageously witnessed to this principle during the Second World War.

80. (John) was in the deserts

Doing what? Ever since the world of scholarship learnt of the discovery of the great library of scrolls at Qumran, on the shores of the Dead Sea, there has been speculation whether John might have lived there until his ministry began. Perhaps his aged parents died when he was tiny, and the community of Qumran, with its special veneration for the priesthood, might have adopted him. The Judaean desert is certainly a large area; but there is nothing in Luke against the hypothesis, and a little to support it, namely John's asceticism and his baptismal practice—though John's baptismal doctrine ('for the forgiveness of sins' NEB—3.3) does not accord with that of Qumran. The immense value of a period of preparation in the desert has been proved by other religious leaders, and it is normal in that remarkable modern order, the Little Brothers of Charles de Foucauld.

2.1. all the world should be enrolled

Since Quirinius did not go to Syria until after the death in 4 BC of King Herod (who is still alive at 1.5), but was responsible for a census in AD 6 (cf. Acts 5.37), it is sometimes held that this story of a universal census is a literary device to get Joseph and Mary from their home at Nazareth to Bethlehem in order that the evangelist may describe the birth of Jesus as a fulfilment of the prophecy of Micah (quoted by Matt. 2.6). But in spite of the difficulties of extricating the factual, dateable, elements in a narrative (chs 1-2) which is essentially theological interpretation, and the disadvantage (?) that Luke was an evangelist and not a professional historian with access to official documents, it seems that Luke may only have made a mistake about the name of the governor and the scale of the enterprise. Most probably the census was a local affair ordered by the emperor and carried out by Herod in co-operation with Sentius Saturninus, a governor before Quirinius, and this is in fact asserted by Tertullian (died 220). Papyri found in Egypt testify to the instructions about returning to ancestral homes.

4. Nazareth

Apart from the evangelists, there is not a single extant author until the third century who so much as mentions Nazareth. 'Can any good come out of' so contemptible a place (John 1.46)?

7. first-born

This is not an implication that there were later children of the marriage. It does indicate that, in accordance with the OT, Jesus would have a special status in the family.

8-13. shepherds

It is not known in what month Jesus was born. December 25th has been observed as Christmas Day since the fourth century when the festival was established in Rome as a Christian alternative to the pagan festival of the sun observed since 274 on the same day. But it is known that from March to November sheep were kept out in the pasture grounds of Judaea; and shepherds of Bethlehem who were minding them were the first of humankind to be told the news. They promptly go and worship the Son of David, the Chief Shepherd, who is to feed his sheep (Ezek. 34.23).

'The Lord's Christ' (i.e. Yahweh's anointed one, Messiah) is a frequent expression in the OT, but here Christ is *identified* with the Lord (as also by Peter at Pentecost, Acts 2.36).

14. on earth peace, good-will toward men (AV)

Familiar words, but it needs to be emphasized that the peace and the good-will are God's: they are the gifts of God which come from his act of reconciliation in Christ. However, if, with RV, we follow the best Greek manuscripts, GOOD-WILL goes into the genitive: the peace is given to men 'of God's good pleasure', or IN WHOM HE IS WELL-PLEASED, i.e., the true children of God, because he has chosen them. The manuscript evidence is confirmed by finding that a similar expression is used in the almost contemporaneous Dead Sea Scrolls.

21. for circumcising him

Circumcision had long been practised among the Jews, and since the Exile in Babylon (which began in 586 BC) it had become a religious and national obligation differentiating the Jews from their neighbours. So, like John, Jesus ('Yahweh is helper') was born 'under the law' (Gal. 4.4) and he rendered obedience to it, because it was not abrogated until the new covenant was sealed.

22-32. their purification

Forty days after Jesus' birth, when the purification days had in their case been completed, and Mary was free to travel, they all make the journey to the capital, some six miles to the north of Bethlehem, and Jesus enters the Temple for the first time: the climax of the Lucan infancy narrative. Normally the sacrifice of a lamb was the rule for a purification sacrifice; but in the case of those who could not afford this expense, two turtle-doves or young pigeons were permitted instead. It is not actually stated that this sacrifice was offered and it has been suggested that the family was exempted on account of Levitical relations; in which case the presentation of Jesus is Luke's substitute for the sacrifice. More probably, the sacrifice is not mentioned because its purpose in the narrative is only to specify the occasion for Jesus' first entry into the Temple.

Jesus' arrival in the Temple evokes from Simeon a canticle, full of OT allusions, which announces that with the coming of Messiah the old order is to be superseded. Simeon represents Israel's Journey's End. In the East it is commemorated by a feast called The Meeting (*Hupante*).

Three striking expressions are used by Simeon. In Jesus SALVATION has come (30). In the Greek OT the words 'salvation' and 'saviour' are used (of God) some 35 times, and it is obvious from their repeated use in Luke 1 and 2 that Christians soon referred them to Jesus.

In verse 32, Simeon borrows an expression from one of the Servant passages in Second Isaiah and calls Jesus A LIGHT . . . TO THE GENTILES; and THE GLORY OF THY PEOPLE ISRAEL, a description reserved in the OT for God alone.

In 35, Simeon prophesies A SWORD through Mary's heart, which can refer both to Mary as the mother of Jesus (who would suffer anguish on Good Friday) and also to Mary as the Virgin Daughter of Sion, and nation of Israel, for Jesus will bring bitterness and anguish to the nation too (cf. Ezek. 14.17): his word will be a sharp sword, like that of the Servant in Isa. 49.2, to pierce the heart of Israel, dividing the Jews into those against him and those who would be RISING (34) with him to newness of life.

36. Anna

ANNA had earnestly prayed that she might see the Messiah—like the woman whose crying night and day for justice is given as an example to the Church to persevere in prayer in face of the Messiah's second coming (18.7 f.). Anna prayed for the coming of Messiah as her OT name-sake prayed for the coming of Samuel (I Sam. 1), and just as Hannah presented Samuel to the Lord, and he 'grew on, and was in favour both with the Lord, and also with men', so it is with Jesus (40). And just as Hannah and

Elkanah went home to Ramah, so Mary and Joseph return to Nazareth.

41-51. *Jesus in the Temple*

Every Jewish child was interrogated about his religion at the age of twelve; it was a kind of confirmation service. But Jesus, instead of answering questions, put questions to the teachers! Luke writes the story of the first Passover of his Gospel so that it deliberately anticipates the last. There are questions in the Temple, the absence of Jesus, his reappearance *after three days*. Mary and Joseph are astonished, the disciples will be bewildered; do they not realize that he *must* be in his Father's house, *must* rise again? And there is a journey from Jerusalem . . . to Nazareth . . . to Emmaus.

The infancy narrative thus ends with the unique son in his Father's house, which is no surprise after 1.32, 35, and Gospels being the sort of books they are it is no surprise to be warned at the beginning of the Passion at the end.

A note on the Virgin Birth of our Lord

There is a kind of puerile apologetic which tries to save the evangelist's reputation as an historian and at the same time relieve the alleged difficulties of modern people about the miracle by calling attention to the phenomenon known to biologists of parthenogenesis—as though the credit of a supernatural gospel could be saved by excluding the supernatural; by classifying the birth of Jesus among the curious reproductive systems of the apiary. This will not do. Luke is saying that the entry of Jesus into the world was attended by mystery as was his death, and that the power which split the Temple veil and rolled away the stone also fertilized an ovum of Mary. The Virgin Birth therefore cannot be demonstrated by historical research to have happened or not to have happened.

But historical criticism can clear the ground for faith. For example, historical criticism can refute the attempts

that have been made in the past to show that the Virgin
Birth did not form part of the earliest tradition. It was
pointed out, quite correctly, that the story is not in the
earliest Gospel (Mark) or in the epistles of St Paul, and
probably not in the Fourth Gospel. But silence does not
itself denote ignorance. It is noticeable for example that
Mark 6.3 calls Jesus 'son of Mary', whereas a Jew would
normally use the father's name. Matthew (13.55) can change
Mark's oddity to 'son of the carpenter' without risk of
misunderstanding because he has an infancy narrative. St
Paul's letters are too occasional in their matter for any
conclusions to be drawn from their lack of references. (Or
does his 'new Adam' include the notion that Christ
resembled the first Adam in owing nothing to a human
father?) St John in I John 5.18 appears to mean that a
new birth is a practical possibility for Christians because
it could be said specifically of Christ that he was in a
unique sense 'born of God'.

A more serious objection to accepting the story has
always been the possibility that Luke found the idea in a
non-Christian source and applied it to Jesus as a way of
commending his Gospel to a Hellenistic world with a taste
for marvels. Was Heracles begotten by Zeus? The Christian had no need to feel inferior. Did the Jew not owe
his very existence to the remarkable pregnancies of elderly
women? The New People of God could also tell of a
miraculous origin. So it might be argued. Yet, the pagan
portents (thunderbolts and snakes) are in a different class
from the reticent narrative of Luke. And the OT births,
however much they may have been in Luke's mind as he
wrote, are in fact NOT virgin births. Isa. 7.14 (in the
Hebrew) probably does not refer to a *virgin* and certainly
does not mention the action of the Spirit and cannot have
given rise to the belief. The Jews did not expect the
Messiah to be born of a virgin, whatever the Greek trans-
lators of Isa. 7.14 meant by *parthenos*.

According to Gen. 1.2 the Spirit of God brought the
world into existence out of the primeval waste, and Luke
is stating that at the renewal of creation the same Spirit
is again at work. And the real question is the doctrinal
one: whether the narrative is to be regarded as the necessary means of expressing this truth for Hellenistic Jews
and is devoid of historical value, or whether the Virgin
Birth was itself the necessary means of inaugurating the
New Creation, as the Catholic Church has always maintained.

The historical Christian view regards the miracle, first,
as the *corollary* of the doctrine of the Incarnation. There
was a definite break in the chain of sinful human life:
there was, literally, a new creation. Secondly, the story is
a defence of the doctrine against the heresy of Adoptionism;
for if Joseph was his father, Jesus must at some point of
time have been 'adopted' into the Godhead, raised to the
level of deity (e.g. at the ascension), which is not the same
doctrine as God taking human flesh. The gospel narrative
also excludes the heresy of Synergism, that God and man
co-operate in the process of salvation. For man is passive,
receptive and obedient to the activity of God.

Karl Barth argued in favour of the miracle on the ground
of its accordance with God's method. For the sovereignty
of the human will which is characteristic of natural life
and which is particularly expressed by the masculine rôle,
is here banned. Man in his pride and defiance is compelled
to retire into the background in the impotent figure of
Joseph. On the other hand, some theologians reject the story
of the Virgin Birth on the ground that it conflicts with the
genuineness of the Lord's humanity: is there not here a
touch of docetism—the heresy that Christ's human nature
was a mere appearance? A true human being must have
both masculine and feminine genes. Moreover the doctrine
'has frequently served to strengthen ascetic anti-sex ten-
dencies, quite apart from the fact that it has become a main

support of Mariolatry, which is so entirely foreign to the Bible '.[1] But, as Dr Alan Richardson says (*Introduction to the Theology of the New Testament*, p. 171), the emphasis on the reality of the *birth* argues anti-docetism.

While therefore there need be no refusal of this story for anyone who is prepared to concede the possibility of the operation of the Transcendent upon the created order, the difficulty of the question makes it inevitable that some modern readers will be conscientiously unable to draw the line between history and theological interpretation exactly where, say, St Thomas Aquinas drew it. The relation between history and interpretation in the gospels is extremely difficult.

The importance of Jerusalem in the Lucan writings

In contrast with the other synoptists, Luke shows an immense, but ambivalent, interest in Jerusalem. Altogether it is mentioned no less than 96 times in Luke-Acts. To Jerusalem (only in Luke) comes Jesus twice in the first two chapters; only in Luke's version of the Transfiguration scene does the conversation refer to Jesus' coming 'exodus' in Jerusalem; the central section of Luke, one of the special features of the third Gospel, starts off in 9.51 with heavy emphasis on the journey to Jerusalem, and at intervals the reader is reminded of the sombre destiny of this journey, until in 18.31-3 there is an explicit prediction of the Passion. In 19.41 ff. (only in Luke) Jesus weeps over the city when he foresees how its enemies will destroy it. Then, after the guilt of the leaders of the people has been exposed, there follow in 24.1-49 a series of appearances of the Risen Lord which Luke (and only Luke) confines to Jerusalem and its neighbourhood. In 24.50 the Ascension takes place at Bethany, after which the apostles

[1] E. Brunner, *Dogmatics*, II, 1952, p. 355. (This is too sweeping. But there remain grounds for disquiet as long as it is suggested by Roman Catholic theologians that the full gospel to be rediscovered by other Christians includes the development in Mariology of quite obscure and casual phrases in scripture.)

return to Jerusalem. The Acts opens (1.8) with a forecast
of the gospel's progress from Jerusalem to the end of the
world and with the descent of the Holy Spirit at Pentecost.
And how the gospel does in fact travel from the capital
of the Jews to the capital of the Empire is the principal
theme of Acts, though not the only one; for it is also
shown that Jerusalem is the place where St Paul not only
starts out but also repeatedly returns, until, in the status
of a 'witness' (Acts 22.15), like the twelve (Acts 1.8), he
finally goes up like his Master to his Passion (20.24; 23.11).

It would seem that Luke is making a theological point.
In the OT Jerusalem is both the holy city, beloved of God,
the city pre-eminently of the prophets and of the king
himself, and also the city whose ill-fortune it was always to
reject the prophets who were sent to her (Luke alone adds
the words 'and all the prophets' at 13.28). Luke would
show that it is exactly so with the greatest of the prophets
(13.33) and the rightful king of Israel (23.2, RV marg.).
He also is rejected by the city which he loves (13.34);
he too comes to receive the throne of his father David, but
is condemned by the leaders of his people. And the
immediate consequence must be the extinction of this holy
but apostate city (only Luke, in 21.24, mentions that
Jerusalem itself would be destroyed) and then the Church's
mission to the Gentiles (13.29-30). Old Israel must be
replaced by the Christian Church. Nevertheless there
remains hope for the Jews. St Paul said in the epistle to
the Romans that the replacement of the Jews did not signify their final and utter rejection (note Rom. 11.26), and
in II Thess. 2.3-12 he seems to expect Jerusalem to be the
scene of the future destruction of antichrist. Luke may be
hinting at the same happy, ultimate end when Anna speaks
of Jesus TO ALL THEM THAT WERE LOOKING FOR THE RE-
DEMPTION OF JERUSALEM (2.38), and when, after the
Resurrection, the apostles are able to re-enter the city
WITH GREAT JOY (24.52).

III

JESUS' BAPTISM

3.1-23a

Whereas Matthew is content with a simple 'And in those days', Luke indicates when the Lord's ministry began with an elaborate attempt to fix the date in the manner of Thucydides or Josephus. But Luke had no public library in which to verify these facts, and there is a problem. The fifteenth year of Tiberius could be either 28-29 (from the death of Augustus) or 26-27 (from the time when he was first associated with Augustus as joint ruler). The other personages fit either date. But Lysanias who is mentioned by Josephus and on inscriptions was probably ruler of Abila, a town of Lebanon (modern Suk), not Abilene, and Annas had been deposed by the Romans. (He may have retained the title, like modern ecclesiastics *emeriti*, since he could argue that the high-priestly office was for life, and no doubt he gave advice to his five sons and his son-in-law Caiaphas, who all in turn occupied the office.)

Some kind of baptismal rite has been common in religions everywhere and though water was a precious commodity in Palestine, the Jews were no exception. They had their rites of purification, e.g. if one touched a corpse (Tob. 2.5); and Josephus, the Jewish historian, tells of his teacher Banus who bathed every morning and every night in cold water. But Josephus reserves the title 'the Baptizer' *par excellence* for John, and evidently the hostility of Herod was aroused by the association of his baptism with a lively expectation of the immediate coming of some sort of Messianic kingdom. Herod feared the gathering of a revolutionary army. John's baptism is for the remission of sins in view of the coming one who is to follow John. The verb used in Greek is in the intensive form and denotes more than just dipping or even washing. In Isa. 21.4 the word is used for 'horror has *appalled* me' (RSV), i.e. submerged me. John's baptism was an acted parable, such as the OT prophets practised: the repentant sinner was submerged, drowned as it were, to mark the end of the old life.

But why did John choose to express this idea by baptism? Possibly he had in mind the cleansing of Naaman in the Jordan; possibly he acted under the influence of the Qumran community in which a threefold immersion in running water was the ceremony of initiation, used after the candidate had taken an oath of loyalty to the Torah of Moses, corroborated by a visible change in his way of life. (John however did not baptize people into a corporate and ascetic fellowship of believers, but when they had been purified for the coming judgement he sent them back to their homes.) Or John's baptism was an extension of the Jewish custom of proselyte baptism. All converts to Judaism were required to offer sacrifice (until the destruction of the Temple made this impossible), to be baptized, and (in the case of male converts) to be circumcised. In this case 'John says in effect: You call yourselves Jews, you claim to be the descendants of Abraham, you demand the privileges that belong to Israel. You have no right to the name, no right to the status; you have forfeited all by your wickedness. You have only one chance. You must begin where the unclean Gentile begins—at the bottom. You must re-discover, and re-learn your Judaism from the beginning. Only so can you hope to have any part in the good time that is coming' (T. W. Manson, *The Servant-Messiah*, 1953, pp. 44-5).

In vv. 4-6 John quotes Isaiah 40. The coming salvation will be the Messianic redemption, and it will be offered to all mankind. But not everyone will see the 'glory'; hence Luke omits Isa. 40.5a but includes 5b.

7. wrath

The wrath of God is frequently mentioned in the OT and is sometimes dismissed as a piece of irrational anthropomorphism which should have no place in Christian theology. But a glance at a biblical concordance will show how often the wrath comes also in the NT. In the Gospels our Lord is sometimes portrayed as righteously angry; the wrath is an essential element in St Paul's thought; and it appears in the book of Revelation, which becomes the more interesting with the increasing support for the view that Revelation is from the same hand as the rest of the Johannine literature. The epistles of John have much to say about the love of God; and the wrath is indeed the corollary of the love of God: it is because God loves man and has called him into fellowship with himself that inevitably the rejection of that fellowship must lead to man's perdition—which is an operation of the wrath, as Julian of Norwich and other mystical writers, like William Law, have explained. It is not an *irrational* passion at all.

The wrath of God can be modernized by describing it (with Dr C. H. Dodd, *The Epistle to the Romans*, 1932, p. 23) as 'an inevitable process of cause and effect in a moral universe'. But if God is the Creator of this moral universe, he is still ultimately responsible for such effects, and the Bible is aware of this when it reports the words of God, 'I make peace, and create evil; I am the Lord, that doeth all these things' (Isa. 45.7). Cf. P. T. Forsyth:[1] 'Sin, hell, curse, and wrath! . . . O you may correct the theology of it as you will, but you cannot wipe—not all the perfumes of progress can hide—the reality of these things from the history of the soul, nor from its future.

[1] Like Dr Dodd, Dr Forsyth, who died in 1921, was a Congregationalist; as a theologian he anticipated the movement in Protestantism associated with Dr Karl Barth.

They abide with us because the Holy Father will not leave us, because grace is the "hound of heaven". They are a function of that holiness which is life's own ground of hope.'

8. It is no use trusting that the merits accumulated by Abraham and the Fathers could be drawn on to tip the balance when someone's individual merits are judged just too little!

14. Hardly soldiers of the Roman army: more probably Jews, offensively lax to their neighbours, who were available to protect and assist the *publicani* (12) in their unpopular work of collecting the taxes required by Rome.

16. to unloose

According to Matthew (3.11) the Baptist speaks of 'carrying' (RSV) Jesus' shoes; one of the duties of a slave that a disciple was expected to do for his Jewish teacher. Mark, Luke (and Acts 13.25) and the Fourth Gospel represent the Baptist as even willing to *take off* Jesus' shoes—one of the slave's duties that a Jewish disciple was exempted from.

Jesus' gift of baptism with Spirit (Hebrew *ruach*, whose literal meaning is wind) and with fire took place at Pentecost. In the OT (Mal. 3.2) there is a promise of purification by fire, and in the *Manual of Discipline* (one of the Dead Sea scrolls) it is said that God will purify by a holy spirit. Luke combines both notions.

17. whose fan

The FAN is the 'winnowing shovel with which the farmer throws the grain against the wind to separate it from the chaff' (Creed), or a fork. Christ will be the great Winnower to separate evil from good.

20. in prison

According to Josephus, John was imprisoned in a fortress near the Dead Sea, at Machaerus. The account of John's death may be read in Mark 6. But Mark 6.17 is wrong in naming Philip, the brother of Herod Antipas, as the previous husband of Herodias. Philip was her son-in-law. Luke 3.19 has therefore corrected Mark.

21. when all the people were baptized

But among the crowds who went 'confessing their sins' (Mark 1.5) was Jesus, and *his* baptism is the historic link between the eschatological baptism of John and the baptism into the death and resurrection of Christ of Rom. 6.1-11.

Mark 1.5 might have been misunderstood to imply that Jesus was conscious of sin, and Matthew adds John's protest (3.14), and so guards against the error, while the fourth evangelist omits the scene altogether. (Their embarrassment is good evidence of the historicity of the event itself. The Church was not likely to invent it.) In actual fact, Jesus could no doubt not stand aside from the purified and purifying nucleus that John was creating and there was no question of his being conscious of sin.

As in the birth, the Holy Spirit, symbolized by the dove, IN A BODILY FORM (22) (i.e. 'in a manner wholly unlike the often transient inspiration of an ordinary prophet' G. W. H. Lampe), is making something new: for the manifestation of Messiah marks a fresh stage in the new creation. (There was a Jewish saying that the Messiah would not become known until he had been anointed by Elijah, and anointing was often regarded as the sacramental means of imparting the Spirit. Cf. I Sam. 10.1, 6, 10; Acts 10.38.)

Bath qol (=the divine utterance; literally, daughter of the voice) was a common Rabbinic way of designating a revelation from heaven, to a teacher perhaps, and was regarded as 'an inferior substitute for inspiration by the Holy Spirit', such as the prophets enjoyed (C. K. Barrett, *The Holy Spirit and the Gospel Tradition*, 1947, p. 40). But the words uttered show that Jesus has more inspiration than that of a teacher and of a prophet combined. The words are a rough quotation from the Servant Song in Isa. 42.1, and the voice therefore would be taken by Luke to mean: 'Thou art not being baptized for thine own sins, but for the sins of the whole people': or, as Matthew puts it, the baptism of Jesus was 'to fulfil all righteousness', to win the redemption of mankind. Because this redemption was consummated on Calvary, it can be held that the voice represents the commissioning of Jesus, so that from now on in the Gospels the words 'to be baptized' come to be a metaphor simply for Jesus' sacrificial death (as in 12.50). And if Jesus' descent into the waters foreshadows the passion, his ascent to receive the Holy Spirit foreshadows Pentecost.

It is not so easy to go back beyond what the words meant for Luke and to ask what significance the baptism had for Jesus, but it seems not improbable that for him too the baptism was an identification of himself with his people, and if John was indebted to Qumran, Jesus' association with John may have led him from that moment onwards to conceive his mission in terms of the Suffering Servant. For the community at Qumran probably looked to itself, or to an individual within the community, becoming the embodiment of the servant ideal; and almost certainly it was in these terms that the Lord understood his work.

One word in the utterance which is not derived from Isa. 42.1 is SON, which comes from Ps. 2.7 (one manuscript actually substitutes the whole verse here), which was one of the OT passages occasionally used by the early Church to prove that Jesus was Messiah, the person through whom God's promises to Israel would be fulfilled. But when the Church moved out into the Gentile world, the title had a new interest. The Jewish-Christian terminology was of Jesus' *function*, in terms of history. Jesus was doing God's work: the coming of the Kingdom was *God's* bringing of the Kingdom. The Greeks however would ask about Jesus' metaphysical relationship to God, and the Church, as early as I Thess. 1.9 f. could affirm his divine status by using the term 'Son of God', an OT term which would have more meaning for Gentiles that 'Christ' (Messiah), which sank to the level of a mere proper name (Jesus Christ).

23. thirty years of age

Luke is careful to point out that the Son of David began his ministry at the same age as king David began his reign (II Sam. 5.4). The words AS WAS SUPPOSED serve to remind the reader that the genealogy traced through Joseph does not conflict with the fact of the virgin birth. As it happens, neither Matthew nor Luke traces the descent from David through Mary: descent on the mother's side carried with it no right of succession and when Joseph accepted Mary's supernaturally conceived child, he conferred upon Jesus the legal rights of sonship. The authenticity of Joseph's claim has been disputed on the ground that in the second century BC the leadership of the Maccabees from the house of Levi was never challenged by members of the house of Judah: so could they have still existed? This is true. But members of the Davidic house did carefully cherish their genealogy and traditions, since we know that several of them confessed it later on before the emperor Domitian. It is not impossible that the Davidic family continued to reside in Persia after other Jews had returned to Palestine; and that the grandparents of Joseph decided to emigrate at last like the OT heroes at the time of Zerubbabel, though this is mere speculation. Nearer to historical reality is the rôle of James *the Lord's brother*: he seems to have assumed leadership of the Mother Church (cf. Acts 15.13) in virtue of his blood relationship to Jesus and this presidency may well have been regarded by the Jewish-Christians as part of the fulfilment of the prophecies about the Davidic dynasty.

JESUS' GENEALOGY

3.23-38

The genealogies given by Matthew and Luke do not coincide. Matthew begins with Abraham and describes three sets of fourteen generations; it was natural for Christians, so conscious of the *third day*, to think of the kingdom of Christ coming after the third span. In Luke the basic number is seven, and the total number of generations is 11×7, but he too, going right back to Adam, seems to divide his names into three main groups. The divisions between them are marked (as in Matthew) by a captivity: and, we are to remember, each captivity produced a Joshua (Jesus in Greek)—Joshua who led the Israelites into the Promised Land; Joshua, the high priest at the end of the Exile; and our Jesus, the third, whose coming is associated with a third captivity (Luke 21.20.24).

Luke is able to make this artificial construction because he traces the names from David to our Lord through Nathan, Solomon's brother, and so is not tied to the scripture. The point of it is a theological one: he makes only eleven groups (or 'weeks', Dan. 9.25 etc.) of seven, and, just as eleven apostles was an incomplete number, and needed to be completed (Acts 1.26), so eleven 'weeks' leave room for one more—the time before the end, the time in which the gospel is to be preached to all nations, the era of the Church of Christ.[1]

Matthew has put his genealogy (Matt. 1.1-17) at the beginning of the infancy narrative, whereas Luke has it in the middle of a series of events which all provide evidence of Jesus' Messiahship: Jesus is Son of Adam, destined to undo the evil consequences of the first Adam, as portrayed in the Genesis myth. St Paul refers to Christ as 'the last Adam' in I Cor. 15.45.

IV

THE TEMPTATIONS

4.1-13

In its preaching to the Jews and in its own rational thought about the Messiahship of Jesus, the early Church felt sure that an historical pattern had been set in the OT to which the life of the Christ was bound to conform, and, in this, they were but reproducing what they had learnt from Jesus himself. The basic facts of Israel's national life were those mighty acts of God by which he chose a special people, redeemed them from slavery and gave them the promised land for a possession; and the prophets thought that any future acts of redemption might be expected to repeat in substance the same cycle of events. It was an interpretation of history, an assertion of the consistency of God's purpose. So when the Redeemer at length did come, his life-story was understood in terms of the classic cycle of past redemptive history; it was, in fact, the climax of that history in a form which fulfilled Israel's mission.[1]

Just as Israel was 'baptized' in the Red Sea (I Cor. 10.2), so was Jesus in the Jordan. If the old Israel had then toiled for forty years in the wilderness and yielded to the temptation not to trust in God, so the Representative of the New Israel would repeat the ordeal. Only, this time, he must suceed where they failed. So no sooner has he emerged from the waters than he enters upon his forty days' lonely ordeal and is urged by the devil to accom-

[1] L. S. Thornton, *Revelation and the Modern World*, 1950, p. 280; U. Mauser, *Christ in the Wilderness*, 1963.

modate his mission to the mentality of Israel. Thus, the Chosen People had constantly in their history attempted to extend God's frontiers by the sword: but the Beloved Son, from the moment of his baptism, was pledged to let evil do its worst to him, and defeat it by accepting it. That is the background for the temptations.

Son of God? And yet must take upon himself the rôle of the Suffering Servant? If Moses had averted a crisis at Massah by producing water from a rock, why should not Moses' successor produce food from THIS STONE? Why not put God to the test and oblige him to demonstrate that the status Jesus accepted was no illusion? In 'the day of temptation in the wilderness' Israel doubted—yet was fed. The Lord by contrast does not doubt, will not put God to the test, and knows that bread is not the only necessity for life (Deut. 8.3). Next, he is shown ALL THE KINGDOMS OF THE WORLD and invited to gain their allegiance by means of a compromise. Why not accomplish Israel's mission in a way the people would at once understand? For so great an end—why not cast out devils by Beelzebub? But no. Could he rob God of that sole and absolute authority which the jealous God demanded when he spoke to Moses (Ex. 34.14)? Should he yield to this 'most black and horrid idolatry' (Matthew Henry[1])? He would not: though the temptation may well have recurred during the ministry, perhaps after the feeding of the five thousand, perhaps when the disciples argued their claims for places of honour in the coming kingdom, perhaps when he rode in triumph into Jerusalem like Simon Maccabeus coming home from battle (I Macc. 13.51). The authenticity of Jesus' temptations is vouched for by the epistle to the Hebrews (2.18; 4.15).

Last of all (Luke has altered Matthew's order, so that the visit to Jerusalem is made the climax of the three),

[1] 'Prince of Commentators'; Presbyterian minister at Chester, d. 1714.

Jesus is taken in his imagination to the top of the Temple and encouraged by quotations from scripture itself to demonstrate to the public (and to himself?) that he is the Messiah. For if he threatened to kill himself, would not God be compelled to come to the rescue with his angels? (This was indeed the temptation to which, on Schweitzer's famous theory, Jesus did succumb, when he 'laid hold of the wheel of the world to set it moving on that last revolution which is to bring all ordinary history to a close. It refuses to turn, and he throws himself upon it', *The Quest of the Historical Jesus*, p. 369.) It was the temptation to substantiate his claim by a public display of magic, as the Pharisees demanded (Matt. 12.38) and as Herod hoped for (Luke 23.8).

Yet though he resists these temptations to vindicate his claim and to prove his Messiahship, there follow in the narrative three miracles which do in fact show those who have the eyes to see that Jesus is the chosen Son of God. The miracles are placed by Luke in the reverse order to the temptations, according to the device well-known in classical Greek and in the NT (e.g. Rom. 10.9 f.; I Cor. 4.10, 7.3 etc.) of chiasmus (the pattern a b c c b a). Jesus refused to throw himself from the Temple: but when in 4.29 the people of Nazareth try to throw him down from a hill, he miraculously goes his own way. He will not win the world by a compromise with the devil: rather, he expels the devil (4.35, 36) from one of his lodgements as a pledge of Messiah's ultimate victory over the whole world. And while he will not command bread to issue from a stone, Simon's nets in 5.6 win a great multitude of fishes from the obdurate sea. (Another instance of chiasmus in Luke-Acts is that of the geography: in the Gospel the Lord proceeds from Galilee of the Gentiles through Samaria and Judaea, to Jerusalem; in the Acts the good news proceeds from Jerusalem through Judaea and Samaria to the Gentiles.)

AT NAZARETH AND CAPERNAUM

4.14-end

Only Luke mentions Nazareth, and his account of this scene is longer than that of the other synoptists since he adds an account of what Jesus preached. Jesus was no doubt invited in accordance with custom a few days before by the president of the synagogue, and he unrolled the book of Isaiah at 61.1, 2 (which Luke probably quotes from memory), though he ended with the words TO PROCLAIM THE ACCEPTABLE YEAR OF THE LORD, leaving out 'and the day of vengeance of our God', presumably deliberately. But whereas people were willing enough to hear a general exposition of the blessings of the Messianic Age, it was a different matter when they were taunted with unpatriotic notions from the prophets; when the coming of the Messianic Age was somehow identified (THIS SCRIPTURE HATH BEEN FULFILLED, 21) with the humble teacher who now SAT (20) before them and whose parents ('*as they supposed*', 3.23) were their own neighbours. From admiration the congregation turned to anger, and the mob intended to lynch Jesus. There is a hill about fifty feet high which directly overhangs Nazareth and on it today are a school and a Roman Catholic church.

23. Physician, heal thyself

Jesus forecasts that they will reproach him with this proverb when they hear what things he has done elsewhere. 'Establish your claims by evidence that we can see.' It was again the demand for a sign.

25-30. This is Luke's second addition to the story, and it is a piece of tradition about Jesus that forehadows what

will frequently be said of St Paul in the Acts. Unacceptable in his own country (24), the apostle, like Elijah and
Elisha before him, will turn to the Gentiles.

31. Capernaum

A synagogue of the third century AD was unearthed at
Capernaum (Tell Hum) after the first world war and partly
restored by members of the Franciscan order.

33. a spirit of an unclean devil

Nervous or mental illnesses are ascribed in the NT to
the agency of demons. So also is the woman's disease at
13.11. By exorcism, they are cast out by Jesus and the
sufferers healed, but in certain cases the demons explicitly
recognize Jesus and his superior power. Here they rightly
guess that Jesus has come to destroy them: his whole
work could be described in terms of conflict and victory
over the demons.

41. he suffered them not to speak

The demons are enjoined to keep silence about Christ
(cf. 35 above). Jesus makes the same demand at other
times, as after certain miracles (Luke 8.56) and after Peter's
confession (9.21). And on the basis of these injunctions a
famous theory of the purpose of the Gospels was built
by sceptical critics.[1] It was an attempt to show that the
Gospels were the early Church's answer to a difficulty: if,
as Christians were convinced, Jesus claimed to be the Son
of God—Messiah—how did it come about that his status
was not eagerly admitted during his ministry? The answer
given by the Gospels, according to this theory, was that
Jesus forbade those who made the discovery to publish it.
Jesus' Messiahship was known by the demons (with their
supernatural insight), but it was unrecognized by men. It
was a secret—until after the Resurrection. Mark's Gospel

[1] Notably by William Wrede in 1901.

accounts in this way for the historical fact that the Messiah-ship of Jesus was only recognized after the Resurrection, but it is done at the price of inconsistencies in the narrative. Thus, obviously Jesus in fact taught the people in parables in order that they might the better understand: but Mark explains that it was a device to conceal the truth from them! The disciples were taken by surprise when the Passion came, yet Mark is obliged to hold that Jesus knew exactly what was to happen and that he gave warnings of it. The disciples are credited with a dullness even beyond the normal among countrymen.

The theory gave an impetus to New Testament studies but was never accepted in Great Britain. It seemed to extract too much from the Resurrection narrative. The disciples' conviction of the Resurrection is made to account for their Messianic convictions (which does not necessarily follow), and indeed for the whole rise of Christianity. But what, on the theory, could have accounted for the dis-ciples' conviction about the Resurrection? 'The elephant stands on the tortoise; but what does the tortoise stand on?' asked Dr William Sanday of Oxford.

It is far better to take the usual English view that the commands recorded in the Gospels about secrecy were, historically, the precautions taken by Jesus to allow his Messianic work of vicarious suffering to be fulfilled. Messiahship was such an explosive concept, and it was bound to be misunderstood—even by disciples. So our Lord required the utmost caution. There was a secret; but it was not a doctrinal invention of Mark; it was a necessity of the mission of Jesus in case his work of redemptive suffer-ing be cut short by patriotic zeal.

What then are we to say about what actually happened when Jesus met the demoniacs if we reject the view that Mark has put words into their mouths which they never uttered? This, with Dr Paul Tillich: 'People far below the average can have flashes of insight which the masses and even the disciples of Jesus do not have: the profound anxiety produced by the presence of Jesus reveals to them in a very early stage of his appearance his messianic character. The history of human culture proves that again and again neurotic anxiety breaks through the walls of ordinary self-affirmation and opens up levels of reality which are normally hidden' (*The Courage to Be*, 1952, p. 63).

40. when the sun was setting

After 6 p.m., when the Sabbath ended, people would be free to travel and to carry.

It is curious that Luke, usually concerned to mention the prayer of Jesus, in 42 omits the reference made by Mark (1.35).

43. therefore was I sent

I WAS SENT is an aorist passive in Greek, derived from the verb which gives us 'apostle'. As the Son is the Father's Apostle, so the Twelve (a corporate body into which St Paul is later added by a special divine operation) are the Son's Apostles, acting with his authority and representing his Person.

V

THE CALL OF SIMON PETER

5.1-11

In Mark two brothers are casting a net and two are mend-
ing nets: here they are clearing out the sand and the
pebbles. Moreover, Peter and the sons of Zebedee are not
represented as they are in Mark, where they leave everything in response to a simple summons, 'Come ye after
me' (Mark 1.17). In this Gospel there is a miracle which
confronts the three with the astounding and awesome
character of the Lord: a miracle very much like that
recorded in the last chapter of John, where fish are also
caught after a fruitless night at the bidding of Jesus, and
which also leads to a solemn charge addressed to Peter.
(This is one of the many points of contact between Luke
and John. Others are: the name Lazarus; the sisters
Martha and Mary; *two* angels at the Easter sepulchre and
other items of the Resurrection narratives. Such details—
and there are a good many more—add weight to the argument that Luke and John have a theological affinity.[1] Both
have a lively hope of the future Kingdom, but both put as
many elements of the eschatological scheme as they possibly can into the past and the present.) Perhaps this story
originally belonged to the Church's collection of post-
resurrection appearances and Luke has deliberately
associated it with the call of Peter to remind the Church

[1] But it is not likely that our Gospel had been seen by the author of
the Fourth Gospel. If the date suggested on p. 32 for the publication of
Luke is correct, then some, at least, of John may even have been written
before Luke.

how obedience to Jesus is rewarded and to encourage Christian missionaries. Luke could not use it at the end of the Gospel because his plan was to describe only resurrection appearances at or near the capital. If this is the case, then it is John who gives us the original context. It is indeed being more and more agreed that the Fourth Gospel, though it has revised the synoptic framework, does preserve some details of history with great accuracy.

If the rejection of Jesus at Nazareth was meant by Luke to be a grim foreshadowing of the final rejection of Jesus by his own people, then, by contrast, the enormous catch of fish would be seen as a happy augury of the success of the apostles under the leadership of Peter, which Luke was going on to describe in Acts. The Church will grow so rapidly that its capacity to cope with an influx of new members will be near to breaking-point (Acts 6.1-2). Three thousand baptisms in a day (Acts 2.41).

TWO MIRACLES

5.12-26

12. a man full of leprosy

Lepers were forbidden to come near centres of population (Lev. 13.46): so it is not clear how this cure could have taken place IN ONE OF THE CITIES. There seems to be the same difficulty with Mark 1.45. Possibly the scene is at the edge of a city. Leprosy first causes ulcers on the skin; then the hair falls out; then the bones dissolve; and because of the horror felt for the disease lepers were obliged to give warning of their approach by uttering the cry, 'Unclean!' But if a leper thought he was healed, he had to present himself to the priest to have the cure officially authenticated, and then, after appropriate sacrifices (14) he would give him permission to mingle again in human society. The last words of 14 are, in the Greek, 'for a proof to *them*'. The priests? In view of the biblical use of the word for 'proof' or 'testimony' in connection with the acts of God, the cleansed leper was probably to be a witness to the priests of the Messiahship of Jesus—as in Acts 4.33, where the same word is used, the apostles are witnesses to the Resurrection of Jesus. The authorities perhaps took note—and waited.

16. and prayed
One of the seven occasions on which Luke alone records the prayer of Jesus.

17. Pharisees
There were about 6,000 Pharisees; they were the strictest observers of the written and the oral law, and represented Judaism at its best.

the power of the Lord
In Mark the paralysed man is carried up the outside staircase and let down through a hole torn in the flat roof made of rafters with branches laid over, the whole being covered with earth. Luke speaks of TILES, which may be an infiltration of a more luxurious mode of life familiar in Luke's world: it certainly makes the exercise described in 19 a lot more difficult!

24. the Son of man
There has been endless argument about this expression which is common in the Gospels but not in precisely this form anywhere in the Greek OT; and it was plainly regarded by the evangelists as a dogmatic and Messianic title. The question is whether Jesus would have used it in that sense. After all, the Aramaic that Jesus actually used could mean simply 'man' and need not be a title. And

surely an open claim to be the Messiah would be incompatible with the Lord's reticence about his Messiahship?

Two facts stand out as fairly certain. First, this enigmatic title, as it is in the Gospels, must have struck a
Greek as very strange, and could not have been invented
by the early Hellenistic Church. Secondly, the evidence
(its virtual absence from the rest of the NT writings) is
that the title was avoided perhaps because it was especially
associated with the lips of Jesus himself. But granted that
Jesus used the words, what did he mean or claim by them?
Possibly he liked the phrase because it was at once an
expression and a concealment of his status. It was not a
purely Messianic title and so could have been taken by
the casual hearer to be referring to men in general, or as
a peculiar way, borrowed from Ezekiel, of referring to
himself. And yet, without a doubt, there was implicit in
the way Jesus spoke a terrible personal claim. 'Man is
lord of the sabbath' (6.5) might pass: but is *man* able to
forgive sins (5.24)? This would have been a blasphemous
assertion for only God can forgive sins; Jesus, however, is
able to do this, just because he is God's agent in bringing
the Kingdom, and this the intelligent opponents of Jesus
did not fail to notice. (Cf. 14 above.)

Therefore if Jesus used the title because of its ambiguity,
because its elusiveness would excite no popular support
for false Messianic expectations, he did not use it (as was
often suggested in a former generation) as a symbol of his
*un*pretentiousness, as though (Ps. 8.5 was often quoted)
Jesus wanted to be no more than a man among men.
Against the background of Daniel 7, 'Son of Man' was
an extremely pretentious piece of self-description. Even if
the disciples did not see this during the ministry, there is
no doubt that when the Gospels were written, the term,
which occurs over seventy times in the synoptists and more
than ten times in John, denoted the supernatural person
of Jesus. The fact that Son of man is in Daniel a symbol

for the corporate, glorified Israel is consistent with Jesus'
regarding himself as the Servant of the Lord, who in
Deutero-Isaiah is also, sometimes at least, a corporate
figure. 'The saints of the most high' are Jesus: he em-
bodies in his person all that is faithful in Israel. Because
most of the instances are in connection with Jesus' approaching Passion or future Exaltation, the Son of Man
of Daniel's eschatological expectation was being interpreted
in the light of the Suffering Servant of Deutero-Isaiah.
Through his obedience even to the death on the cross, and
only through this, would they be raised to glory. And this
future triumph explains the early use (which has no reference to the Passion or Exaltation) of SON OF MAN in chs
5 and 6: because he was to be enthroned, Jesus could on
occasion exercise his power, his proper power, the power
which belongs to the Kingdom of God, such as in forgiving
sins or manifesting his lordship over the Sabbath. Moreover, besides Daniel and Deutero-Isaiah there may also
lie a reminiscence of Genesis; Man (Adam), instead of
fulfilling his destiny as God's vicegerent and reigning in
the world, fell into sin, and brought suffering and death into
the world. In the Gospels, by contrast, the Son of Adam
par excellence, the Representative Man, who has identified
himself with suffering humanity, conquers Adam's temptation and Adam's death, and is to reign on high, giving the
promise that as in Adam all die, so in the Second Adam
all shall be made alive (I Cor. 15.22).

In Greek SON OF MAN is a literal translation of the
Aramaic, and is as irritatingly baffling as 'the son of the
man' to us. No doubt it was preserved in spite of its unin-
telligibility because of its sacred associations (use by Jesus).
But after a while the Hebrew origins of the term were lost
and another Christian generation began to regard it as
denoting the humanity of the Lord, in contrast to his
divinity which was regarded as expressed by 'Son of
God'.

26. they were filled with fear

Fear is again associated with the adoration of God at 7.16 and several times in the book of Revelation. 'Who shall not fear, O Lord, and glorify thy name?' (Rev. 15.4). Fear can therefore be in the NT an expression of *faith*: believers or sympathizers are often called men 'who fear God'—like Cornelius in Acts 10.2. And lack of fear may indicate rebellion against God, like the judge in the parable of Luke 18.2, 4, or the impenitent thief on the cross (23.40). And cf. Rom. 3.18. There is however a fear from which the gospel releases us—a paralysing fear of death (Heb. 2.15) or of harmful adversaries (Luke 12.4). Yet so crucial are the decisions that we take that we must never cease to *fear* the judge of all the world (Luke 12.5).

THE CALL OF LEVI

5.27-end

The Roman government naturally wished to collect its taxes as cheaply as possible, and one method was to auction the taxation of particular areas, and to award the responsibility for the next five years to the highest bidder i.e. the man who submitted the lowest rate of commission. The successful applicant then arranged for the collection of the taxes and sent them, less his commission, to Rome; very likely he exceeded the stipulated scale, and sometimes he accepted bribes. In any case however the Jewish *publicani* were disliked by their compatriots for collaborating with the occupying power and for their contaminating commerce with Gentile merchants.

27. Levi

Mark adds, 'son of Alphaeus'; while in the first Gospel he is Matthew—which is also the name in Luke's list of apostles in ch. 6 and Acts 1 (and Mark 3.18). Either LEVI had two Semitic names and Matthew was the one by which he was known among the Twelve, or—there were thirteen apostles! See on 22.29.

29. a great feast

Before he follows Jesus, he acts as host at a great reception which causes offence to the champions of ritual purity.

32. to repentance

It is characteristic of Luke to add TO REPENTANCE, words not in Mark or Matthew. Similarly, he alone has the parable of the Lost Coin (15.8-10): even one sinner who repents is of infinite value.

33. The disciples of John fast often

The Baptist's asceticism contrasted with this lavish reception and hostile comments evoked from the Lord a claim for himself quite as remarkable as when he overrode the Sabbath law. For the OT prophets had frequently likened God's action towards Israel to a bridegroom with his bride: and Jesus, in the most natural way, accepts the fact that he is a Bridegroom, while John (according to John 3.29) is the Bridegroom's Friend, a technical term for his representative who made the necessary legal arrangements with a similar representative of the bride.

'In the afternoon before the wedding the bridegroom used to leave his house, which was then occupied by the bride and her attendants; meanwhile he sat among his companions. These were THE SONS OF THE BRIDE-CHAMBER (34). At a signal from the bridegroom he and his companions moved off slowly and ceremonially towards his home, where the bride was awaiting him and where the bridal feast was to be held' (C. L. Chavasse, *The Bride of Christ*, 1940, p. 54). The Church will fast later on, when her

Messiah is gone, as is also assumed by Matthew's 'when ye fast, be not as the hypocrites' (6.16). St Paul recommended a stern personal self-discipline to his converts, and fasting (with SUPPLICATION, 33) was practised by the early Church before important decisions were taken.

36-39. a piece from a new garment

In Mark the situation is of a tear being made worse when an old garment is patched with a piece of unshrunk cloth: i.e., you cannot accommodate the life of the New Age in the old forms of Judaism. Here the parable is changed: you do not tear up A NEW GARMENT in order to mend an old; for the two do not match, and anyway it is a quite ineffective repair: i.e., the new teaching does not accord with Judaism. Moreover, those who are committed to Judaism (39) will not welcome the gospel.

VI

LORD OF THE SABBATH

6.1-11

There can be no doubt that from the Jewish point of view
the action of the disciples was illegal: it was a sort of
threshing. But this is not to say that Jesus was tearing
down old-fashioned and tiresome restraints on human
liberty after the manner of a reformer. He did not come to
reform Judaism. He preferred to heal on the Sabbath, to
work the Father's will (John 5.16-17) on the Sabbath, since
the Jewish Sabbath not only looked backwards by com-
memorating God's rest at the end of the creation, but also
looked forwards as being a day in which one anticipated
the bliss of the Messianic age. Jesus is therefore Lord of
the Sabbath because he is Messiah: and his Messiahship
is for the salvation of mankind (Luke 13.14-17). Those
who understand that with the coming of Jesus the Kingdom of God is being inaugurated are exempted from the
Sabbath commandments, as St Paul taught, and as the
reference to David's action (which took place on the Sabbath, according to the rabbis) here suggests. Nevertheless,
as St Paul also taught, the Law is still binding on Jews,
and if anyone violates the Sabbath for any other reason
than his accepting the Messianic salvation, he sins. An
interesting reading in the Bezan codex, a manuscript of
the fifth to sixth century at Cambridge, records that Jesus
saw a man working on the Sabbath day, and said that he
was blessed if he realized why he possessed this freedom,

but was 'cursed' if he was acting out of mere defiance of the Law. (However, the saying is probably not genuine.)

Although the rabbis taught that the Messiah would be of the house of David, this section, with its parallels in Mark and Matthew, is the sole example in the course of Jesus' ministry of David being used as a 'type' of Christ. The evangelists are in this being faithful to the emphasis of Jesus. There was too much of an aura of nationalism round the idea for it to be of much use to Jesus.

6. on another sabbath

Jesus' enemies (a hint here of the coming Passion) are watching in order to entrap him. He publicly heals a man with a withered hand (a stone-mason, according to one of the apocryphal gospels) after demanding whether it was right to heal or to kill on the Sabbath. But the issue was not one of simple humanitarianism, for there is plenty of evidence that the Pharisees themselves made human and sensible provision for urgent need. Their anger is roused because they perceive the implicit claim of Jesus.

The strict observance of the Sabbath seems to have become easier among orthodox Jews of modern Israel. Thus, a farmer can set a switch before the Sabbath which will automatically milk his cows on the Sabbath itself!

THE CALL OF THE TWELVE AND THE SERMON ON THE PLAIN

6.12-7.1

13. he chose from them twelve

The term APOSTLE has a certain fluidity in the NT, but the writers agree that the Lord appointed twelve men to be with him. According to Matt. 10.5 they were promptly sent

on a mission to Israel; this is not denied by Luke, but he
will later record the sending of seventy others to make it
clear that the salvation of Christ is offered to both Jews
and Gentiles.

15. James the son of Alphaeus

The name ALPHAEUS is too common to infer that James
was the brother of Levi (Mark 2.14). The traditional view
is that he was a cousin of Jesus, Alphaeus having married
a sister of Mary, and in this case he is to be identified with
James, the Lord's ' brother ' of Acts 15.13; 21.18; Gal. 1, who
was martyred in AD 62. The other James (14) was martyred
by Herod Agrippa I (grandson of Herod the Great) in 44
(Acts 12.2). See further on 8.19.

Simon which was called the Zealot

Only Luke explicitly mentions that among the Twelve
was a member of the nationalist resistance group. Possibly
he can do this because the revolt of 66-70 had been crushed
and was being forgotten; the name no longer caused
offence to Gentile readers.

Luke specifically mentions that the sermon was preached
ON A LEVEL PLACE (17), which must be a deliberate alteration of Matthew's ' mountain '. Jesus therefore has to *come
down*—as at the Last Day he will also *come down* to pro-
nounce judgement. Because of this judgement *motif* Luke,
unlike Matthew, records a series of *woes*.

20. he lifted up his eyes on his disciples

The sermon is addressed to the disciples, who are
distinguished from the crowd (19) who were also there.
The ethical teaching appears to be intended only for those
who would belong to the Kingdom—and it is encompassed
by Matthew and by Luke with miracle, which in both
Testaments is one of the signs of a divine revelation.

ye poor

Matthew's 'the poor in spirit' indicates that the godly poor (who suffer oppression, and who trust in God for help) of the psalms are meant. Luke in changing this to YE POOR insinuates a suspicion of material possessions as such. The gentle evangelist can be so stern.

21. ye that hunger now

Matthew's blessing is for those who 'hunger and thirst after righteousness'. Luke's, 'O the good fortune of those who hunger' is a promise of the satisfaction of human needs, but basic *religious* needs are included, especially if Luke has in mind the invitation of Isaiah 55 to buy wine and milk without money. The hunger and tears here alluded to are not exhausted however by reference to outward conditions, for in Israel it is known that man does not live by bread alone, and sorrow goes deeper than the sense of earthly want. The hunger is for God . . . the tears are for the tragedy of sin (cf. Ps. 42.3), and the NOW is the eschatological *now* of men face to face with the coming of Christ.

22. Blessed are ye, when men shall hate you

The time shall come when Christian believers will be expelled from the synagogue.

24-26. Woe unto you

These *woes* are presumably not rebuking the disciples ON A LEVEL PLACE themselves: they are a pronouncement of judgement on their contemporaries idling in the capital, though Christians of all ages have listened to these words as a judgement on churchmen too, especially in 26.

Many readers of the Gospels have been pained by the promise of reward which comes in 23 (and elsewhere in this Gospel, e.g. at 6.35; 14.13 f.; 18.22). Are not the ethically best actions devoid of all self-interest? But (1) in the Gospels a good action is never recommended for the sake of the reward it will bring. Rewards are promised to those who follow Jesus from some other motive, such as 'for my sake (and the gospel's)', (Mark 8.35; Luke 9.24). In the parable of Matt. 25.31-46 those who enter into the joy of the Lord are those who are not even conscious of doing good, still less of aiming at a reward.

(2) Jesus' rewards operate according to no human scale of merit. That at least must be the teaching of the parable of the Prodigal Son and the Labourers in the Vineyard. No reward is ever *deserved*, for 'we are all unprofitable servants' and any reward is really grace.

(3) K. E. Kirk,[1] one of the most distinguished of non-Roman moral theologians, held that a stiff refusal to mention or contemplate rewards leads in life to legalism or to a subtle kind of self-centredness. Such a stern refusal is equivalent to a quest for merit, and psychologically it tends to scrupulosity. 'It turns the mind from God and forces it back upon the self and its own successes and failures' (*The Vision of God*, 1931, p. 145). This acute observation implies that our Lord taught that his disciples were neither to make rewards the goal of their ethical endeavour, nor were they to be so self-righteously shocked by the idea that they felt compelled to frantic efforts to subdue it. They will not strive after some ideal Good, but rather in confidence love their Father in heaven (cf. Isa. 49.4), who alone is Good (Luke 18.19).

32. if ye love them that love you

This saying looks back to 27: Love those who oppose you. It is easy enough to be rewarded for loving those we like; but God's reward is given to those who have renounced these tangible rewards in the flesh and who do their duty without such a hope. You can aim at getting man's reward —then do not expect to receive God's. Jesus is not emphasizing the reward that God gives, but deprecating merely earthly ones.

[1] Anglican Bishop of Oxford; died 1954.

35.   AV: **do good, and lend, hoping for nothing again**

     RV: **never despairing** (i.e., of your heavenly reward)

RV marg.:   **despairing of no man** (i.e., always hoping to recover your debt)

But the literal meaning is: 'hoping for nothing in return', which makes excellent sense. Why not keep it? NEB reads: without expecting any return. This accords precisely with the last words of the parable of the Labourers in the Vineyard (Matt. 20.15): we cannot by our own works establish a claim upon God.

The AV rendering has been used by Christians as a condemnation of usury.

Ye shall be sons of the Most High

All men, in as much as they are created beings, have God as their Father. Yet so different is this relationship when it is re-made by Christ that the NT also speaks of believers' *becoming* sons of God in virtue of the unique Sonship of Christ. We are adopted as God's sons; a new relationship is brought about by God towards sinners—it is called justification—but it is not an individual relationship. Individual believers are sons in virtue of the corporate Sonship of the Christian community. The individual is clothed with the righteousness of Christ because by baptism he is a member of the Body which is thus clothed. Baptism therefore is the initial act of grace in which Christ meets the sinner; it is also the sacrament of the believer's initial act of faith. The new relationship is deepened in the daily life of the Body, but will only be totally perfected and fulfilled at the Parousia. The perfection is still an object of *hope*.

36. Be ye merciful

To the man who is locked up in his prison of self-interest, the God who is merciful to the unthankful and the evil is beyond human understanding. Thus the death of Christ is proof of God's love to those who are being saved, but to others it is foolishness (Rom. 5.7). Luke has noticed however, a difficulty of Matthew's version of this saying, 'Be ye perfect . . .' and so has changed it. See the introduction to this commentary, on the Ethical Teaching.

37. Judge not
The divine mercy must be answered by a corresponding forgiving, uncensorious, attitude on our part.

39. Can the blind guide the blind?
Jesus is making use of some current proverbs. A pupil will never get very far with a blind teacher.

41. why beholdest thou the mote . . . ?
Perhaps these telling aphorisms were the result of memories of the carpenter's shop at Nazareth. The temptations of religious people to overlook their own faults and criticize their neighbours has been unforgettably portrayed by François Mauriac in A Woman of the Pharisees.

43. there is no good tree that bringeth forth corrupt fruit
The fruit of a tree entirely depends on the sort of tree it is. A man's deeds depend on his personal character and belief.

46. why call ye me, Lord . . . ?
Faith without works is dead (but v. 10.42). It was possible for a would-be disciple like the Rich Young Ruler (18.18 ff.) to call Jesus 'Good Master' and yet be reluctant to obey his instructions. It is a stern warning to committed Christians too; but the dismal picture of some exegetes, of the Church as ever on the brink of an abyss and liable to go crashing down in a suicidal apostasy hardly represents the truth of the NT concept of the Church as the Body of Christ, of the Church and Christ as inseparable. But it is true all the same that every generation of Christians has to

re-learn the meaning of discipleship so that worship does not become empty formulae. What does it mean to call Jesus LORD and do what he says in the age of nuclear weapons, racial hatreds and the threatened exhaustion of the earth's natural resources?

48. a foundation upon the rock

Matthew's parable of the dry bed of a Palestinian wadi being suddenly flooded by torrential rain, as is common enough, was a warning against the coming Judgement; it follows an explicit reference to ' that day ' (Matt. 7.22). Luke has altered the parable to make it refer to the Christian's present response to Jesus, and the Palestinian wadi turning to a torrent after a cloudburst has become an (Italian?) river which has overflown its banks; both the presentation and the interpretation of the parable have thus been translated into a Hellenistic environment.

7.1. Like Matthew's Sermon on the Mount, Luke's discourse, which began with the disciples, ends with the crowd. Luke is here following the earlier Gospel.

VII

TWO MIRACLES

7.2-17

2. a certain centurion's servant

Luke has expanded Matthew's account of this incident, and the hesitation of Jesus to enter the house of a Gentile is given a slightly different turn: to the centurion's feeling of unworthiness is added (7) his reluctance to approach Jesus.

8. a man set under authority

As a soldier accustomed to instant obedience, he has no doubt that the Lord's word of command will, even at a distance, be no less effective; and such faith, exceeding anything that Jesus had met among the Jews, is given its reward.

A centurion, in this case probably a native of Italy, was chosen by merit from the ranks, and was superior to the N.C.O's. Nominally he was in charge of a hundred men, and each legion had fifty-nine centurions who were themselves divided into different categories. Plainly they were men of some character.

12. the only son of his mother

Jesus, meeting the cortege, is moved with compassion. There is no mention here of faith, but the incident recalls similar miracles recorded in the OT of Elijah and Elisha: Nain was in fact near the scene of one of them (Shunem). But readers of the Gospel would also have in mind another Resurrection of the only Son of *his* mother.

AN ENQUIRY FROM THE BAPTIST
7.18-35

According to Matt. 11.2 John was in prison.

It is sometimes held that John's message must cast doubt on the story of the Baptism. It is said that now for the first time John begins to wonder whether Jesus might be the Coming One (i.e. Elijah, who was to prepare for the coming of the Messiah) and that Jesus' reply is an invitation to John to go even farther and to see Jesus as himself the Messiah. However, it is better to see John's questions as a *doubt*: Had he been mistaken after all? Was Jesus really the Coming One (Messiah), of whom he spoke in 3.16? By way of reply, Jesus told John's disciples to relate the mighty works that they had seen, not as astonishing prodigies, but as signs of the fulfilment of the OT (Isa. 26.19; 29.18; 35.5; 61.1). He *was* Messiah—but not the kind that John had expected. And if Jesus is Messiah, *John* must be 'Elijah'. Hence the ironical questions which Jesus puts to the crowd about John, whose reputation was enormous, and his following considerable. (His disciples continued an existence independently of the Church for a long time.) Verse 28 is difficult. It can hardly mean that John would be ultimately excluded from the Kingdom, when 'Abraham, and Isaac, and Jacob, and all the prophets' (13.28) are there. But John's role was to prepare for the coming Kingdom, which did begin to arrive *after* him.

29. being baptized with the baptism of John

The people 'acknowledged the justice of God' (Moffatt), for they repented, and received John's baptism, whereas the Pharisees frustrated the purpose of God in so far as it concerned themselves. This verse explains 35 below.

35. wisdom is justified of all her children

If, with one manuscript, we omit ALL, then the meaning

is that Jesus and John, though so different, are yet equally sons of the same divine wisdom, and their works are a sufficient justification. If ALL is accepted, the divine wisdom is vindicated by all who listened to John, like the publicans.

A PHARISEE REBUKED
7.36-50

Has Luke combined two stories? There seem to be certain inconsistencies. The host behaves oddly when he neglects his elementary duties; Jesus is said to turn to the woman in 44, but actually speaks to Simon; the parable of the debtors shows that one loves because much has been forgiven, yet the woman is forgiven because she loved much. On the other hand, a connected narrative can be got in this way: Simon was thinking that the woman's sin made a barrier which godly men should not overlook; but, the parable argues, this is not so. For it is obvious that when a great weight of sin is forgiven, there is in response a great love. The evident love of this woman, therefore, is proof that her great sins have been forgiven her.

There are two other gospel stories which resemble this. In Mark 14, just before the Passion, Jesus was entertained by 'Simon *the leper*' at Bethany and was anointed on the *head* by an unnamed woman, and in John 12 Mary, the sister of Martha and Lazarus, anointed Jesus' feet at Bethany. Luke's WOMAN WHICH WAS IN THE CITY (Nain?), A SINNER, has been identified by Latin Christendom since Gregory the Great (d. 604) with Mary Magdalene (8.2), but this is not suggested by the Gospel itself. Originally these stories may have been a simple account of an act of homage to Jesus by an unknown woman; but, in the course of repetition, other ideas became attached in various ways —hence the three versions. There are too many differences in the stories as we have them for John to have been using our Luke.

VIII

AN ITINERANT MINISTRY

8.1-3

Jesus is accompanied by the Twelve and by some women (the names given differ from those in Mark 15.40, except for Mary Magdalene), of whom one is actually the wife of an official in the Herodian household (cf. Acts 13.1). Luke is inclined to stress the occasions when the 'Establishment' proves sympathetic. But it may have had its disadvantage: for Herod Antipas himself might in this way have had an insight into the popularity of Jesus. Certainly, according to Josephus, he was anxious about possible disturbances arising among the Baptist's followers and he may well have feared this associated movement. So he readily consented to the death of Jesus, and (Acts 12.2) his nephew had the apostle James put to death. Jesus' help from women was perpetuated in the Church's ministry in the form of an order of deaconesses (Rom. 16.1; I Tim. 3.11), but the order lapsed in the sixth century when its members seemed to be sinning like the sons of Levi (Num. 16.10), and was only revived in the nineteenth century.

THE PARABLE OF THE SOWER

8.4-15

The parable of the Sower is abbreviated by Luke, but

some of his alterations are not improvements. ON THE ROCK
(6) where the seed could not grow at all, is less suitable
than the 'rocky ground' (Matthew-Mark), where seed
would germinate and then rapidly wither.

8. a hundredfold

This refers to the return of seeds reaped for seeds sown.

11. Now the parable is this

It is usual today to regard this explanation as coming
from the Church rather than from Jesus, on the ground
that it treats the parable as allegory (in the same way as
pagan myths were treated in the Hellenistic world) and
because the interpretation is so confused. 'The seed is the
Word: yet the crop which comes up is composed of
various classes of people. The former interpretation suggests the Greek idea of the "seminal word"; while the
latter is closely akin to a similitude in the Apocalypse of
Ezra. . . . Two inconsistent lines of interpretation have
been mixed up.' Yet surely Jesus himself would have been
perfectly clear about the meaning.

However, allegory, in which all the details of a story
stand for some other meaning, is not in itself proof of
lateness. There are many allegorical passages in the Bible,
which argues that it was a perfectly usual Jewish medium
of teaching. As for the 'confusion', it is certainly not
noticed by most listeners to the parable, who think of the
unchangeable divine revelation being flung among men of
all sorts. The response is varied, in some cases the Word
being stifled, while at other times there are wonderful fruits
of Christian living.

A note on parables

Although in 8.9-10 Luke has abbreviated the 'shocking'
passage of Mark 4.10-12 he has not altered the meaning or
reduced the obvious difficulty—which is, can it really be

true that Christ taught in parables for the purpose of con-
cealing his real meaning? Surely, we suppose, parables
were the masterly technique of Jesus for imparting truth
about the Kingdom which otherwise would have been
utterly beyond them? William Wrede accepted these words
at their face value but regarded them as Mark's and not
Jesus'. They were the ingenious idea of Mark (making use
of Isa. 6.9-10) to explain to the believing Church why Jesus'
teaching had not been accepted in his lifetime. Mark's
answer: Jesus did teach about the Kingdom, only it was
in parables—so that it should not be understood!

English scholars have rejected the Wrede interpretation
on the ground of its being out of keeping with the whole
NT, and have looked in various directions for a way of
escape from the apparent meaning of Jesus' words. One
famous suggestion was that *so that* (10: RSV) was a misunderstanding of an Aramaic particle which could best be
rendered by a relative pronoun: ' To you is given the secret
of the Kingdom; but all things come in parables to those
outside, *who* see indeed, but do not perceive' (for *if they
did* they would repent, Mark 4.12). Because men are blind,
Jesus would help them with parables. But it is the clause
in Mark that Luke does not reproduce that makes an
objection to this theory: it is almost impossible that it is
not a *final* clause—' lest haply they should turn again '.

A better view is to regard *parable* as meaning (as often
in the OT) *riddle* and to translate ' so that' by ' with the
result that' (since Hebrew thought frequently confused result with purpose). In this case, the sense is that while the
disciples have been given the secret of the kingdom by
revelation, to those outside it still possesses the nature of
a riddle, with the result that they hear the words but do
not understand the analogies. How *can* they understand as
long as they remain outside? But why, we wonder, are they
outside? Perhaps because everything from their birth onwards has conditioned them to make a negative response.

Can we, in fact, in the end avoid determinism? We cannot hold that Jesus spoke parables to prevent people from believing. Yet we are led back to the indirect determinants of heredity and environment, which had the result of preventing them! We may not like it, but this seems to emerge from other parts of the NT too. Miracles reveal the same cleavage: they are only recognized as Messianic signs by those who already have faith. 'A parable, like the pillar of cloud and fire, turns a dark side towards Egyptians, which confounds them, but a light side to Israelites, which comforts them, and so answers a double intention. The same light directs the eyes of some, but dazzles the eyes of others' (Matthew Henry). It is the Holy Spirit who enables us to understand the significance of parables and miracles (Luke 10.21).

The *mystery*, or *secrets*, of the Kingdom: what could not be discovered but only revealed, and which has been revealed, and is now proclaimed by the Church. The Christian mystery is an open secret so that those chosen may accept it. And only a faith given by God could possibly see the power of God in the weakness and unkingly humiliation of the Cross. Isaiah is therefore quoted not to condemn the blindness of those rejected, but to emphasize the wonder of those called to serve God's ultimate purpose of salvation. It is indeed in the mercy of God that unbelievers should be confronted with the Kingdom through the medium of riddles. He does not confront the mockers openly, for that would seal their destiny. Nor does he crush believers into submission, for that would deprive them of faith. Hidden beneath a parable or the stumbling words of a village preacher, or veiled behind the Bread and Wine, Jesus comes to those who have faith. Those outside will NOT perceive him, and they turn ON THEIR WAY (14) with sorrow, or relief, or anger.

THE RESPONSIBILITY OF THE CHURCH

8.16-18

16. putteth it on a stand
A disciple should radiate warmth and convince by his integrity, for (17) Christian truth cannot be kept in the dark, unobtrusive.

18. whosoever hath, to him shall be given
The believer will grow in understanding.

THE BRETHREN OF JESUS

8.19-21

Jesus illustrates for his own personal life the precept he gives in 14.26.

19. his mother and brethren
As early as the third century, there have been writers who have regarded the BRETHREN as the natural brothers of Jesus, children of Mary and Joseph, and this is the usual view of contemporary Protestant exegetes. 'There can be little doubt that the Helvidian view (i.e. that Mary had other children) stands as the simplest and most natural explanation of the references to the brothers of Jesus in the Gospels' (V. Taylor, *The Gospel according to St Mark*, 1952, p. 249). On the other hand the Reformers of the sixteenth century as well as all Catholic exegetes have held that Mary had no other children and that the 'brothers' were either children of Joseph by a former marriage (the eastern view) or (in the west) cousins of Jesus. It is conceded that the NT is not explicit, but there is some evidence to support the 'Catholic' view. Mark 6.3 refers to Jesus'

brothers, James and Joses, but in Mark 15.40 James and
Joses (surely the same pair) are sons of another Mary:
Mary, the wife of Clopas, a sister of the Blessed Virgin
Mary, John 19.25. Clopas is another form of Alphaeus;
Luke 6.15. (But while scripture does not contradict the
'Catholic' view, it does not necessitate it, for as Père Lag-
range recognized, 'the perpetual virginity of Mary is a
dogma based rather on Tradition than on Scripture'.)[1]
James 'the less' (Mark 15.40) is therefore one of the twelve,
a relative of Jesus, and an important personage in the
Acts; and always to be distinguished from James, the son
of Zebedee. But the identification is by no means assured.

A STORM SILENCED
8.22-25

As is well known, sudden fierce squalls are common on
the lake, due to its position amid the hills, and the disciples' boat is put in grave peril—while Jesus sleeps! Luke
(unlike Matthew-Mark) is careful to say that Jesus dropped
off to sleep before the storm began. Obviously the evangelists regard the stilling of the water as a miraculous work
of Jesus, but it has been held that what happened was:
first, Jesus rebuked the elements; then followed, by a
providential coincidence, a calm as sudden as the storm;
lastly, the disciples address to *God* their gratitude, over-
come with awe because he has answered Jesus' prayer so
dramatically. Others will hold that here was an assumption
by Jesus of the divine prerogative mentioned in Ps. 89.9.
In both this and the next section it is relevant that in the
Bible the sea sometimes represents chaos and disorder—
just as in dreams water is often a symbol for dark impulses
at work below the level of consciousness. Hence Rev. 21.1:
the danger is over, salvation is complete.

[1] For further discussion, see J. H. Ropes, *The Epistle of St James*
(International Critical Commentary), 1916, pp. 53-74, who rejects the
view maintained here.

LEGION

8.26-39

The multiplicity of the demons implies that the deranged man was seriously ill. He suffered perhaps from a suicidal mania which led him to frequent the graves of the hillside, and where, according to Mark, he cut himself with stones. The story is told from the point of view of the ancient belief in demon possession and it is not easy to say now exactly what did occur when the man was cured. The swine were apparently frightened and rushed down the slope in panic. Some critics have supposed that a miracle story told of some other healer, in the Hellenistic world, has been attributed to Jesus by the evangelist. The swine were not likely to exist among Jews, and this might seem to support such a view, but it is not conclusive since the inhabitants of the country beyond the Jordan were mostly Gentiles. The three synoptists at any rate regard the cure as a striking victory over the demons who plead with Jesus not to send them into the abyss—but in vain: for the demon-possessed swine are engulfed in the waters, and hurled into the abyss of punishment (cf. Revelation 9).

26. Gerasenes

This is not the only possible reading. The ancient manuscripts are confused and the town intended by Luke was probably Gergesa, which was a little north of the centre of the shoreline, on the eastern side of the lake.

38. the man . . . prayed him that he might be with him

The demoniac, as in Mark, now restored to sanity, asks to accompany Jesus, but is not permitted. Rather, he is to go to his own country and spread the news of what God

had done for him. The usual command to secrecy is reversed by Jesus perhaps because on heathen soil the
Messiahship would not be sufficiently understood to be
misunderstood.

A GIRL OF TWELVE IS HEALED

8.40-56

Jesus now RETURNED—to the Jewish side of the lake, and
there follow two miracle stories: the healing of the
daughter of Jairus, into which is inserted the healing of the
woman with menorrhagia. Luke has simplified the narrative, but without abbreviating it as drastically as Matthew,
though in so doing he has destroyed some of the subtlety
of Mark which he did not need. This is notably the case
with his use of the girl's age.

But why should the girl's age be given at all? Many
readers of the Gospels refuse to see any meaning in the
various numbers mentioned other than the literal one. They
see no elusive significance in the reiterated 'twelve'. Yet
the apparent meaning of Mark 5.42 is very odd. She walked
—*because* she was twelve years old? It is not unreason-
able to try to see if this is Mark's way of teaching something, and an investigation of all the occasions when Mark
uses the little word 'for' (Greek, *gar*) has suggested that
he uses the word to indicate that something has been
implied but not actually stated in the text. She began to
walk: she was twelve years old, *don't you see*? And then
there was the woman who had suffered for TWELVE (43)
YEARS. What then are we to look for beyond the external
meaning of the text? Twelve being the number of the
tribes of Israel, and Jairus being a prominent synagogue
official, argues that the something may be found in the
OT.

The two miracles have in common besides the word
TWELVE, the word DAUGHTER and the emphasis on faith
in Jesus. Now Jeremiah speaks of the healing of the
daughter of my people, while Lamentations, which speaks
of mourning for Sion, refers to her need for bread. Can it
not be then that the healing of the daughter of twelve, who
is to be given bread, and the sufferer of twelve years' pain,
contain the underlying meaning that the restoration of
Israel could come only through faith in Jesus? It is a pity
that Luke has transposed the age of the girl to a matter of
fact position at the beginning of the story, but he does
preserve Mark's account in the next chapter of the feeding
of five thousand men with bread, on Jewish soil, with
(9.17) *twelve* baskets of broken pieces left over, separated
from the miracles of healing by the sending of the *twelve*
apostles (9.1-10).

55. be given her to eat
This is the natural sequence to being raised by Christ:
after baptism—the Eucharist. So the readers of the Gospel
would notice. What Jesus actually meant at the time is not
clear, but there is certainly in the OT a connection between
resurrection and feasting (Isa. 25.6, 8). Thus meals were
already associated with the 'age to come', and this will be
part of the background of the Last Supper. At any rate it
can be said that Jesus' miracles were done not only out of
compassion but also to express in a concrete way the meaning of his preaching. His healings were selective; and in the
present instance, according to 8.51 only Peter, John and
James (those who were afterwards to bear witness with
Jesus' authority) are permitted to see the act of restoration.

IX

A MISSION OF THE TWELVE

9.1-10

The twelve are sent to preach to Israel (Matt. 10.6) and to heal. Mark's version (6.8) of the instructions allows a staff; but Luke follows Matthew in rejecting even this modest piece of equipment. When they encounter opposition, they are to shake off the dust, presumably to indicate that the inhabitants were ' as Gentiles and publicans ' (Matt. 18.17), for the Jews regarded even the soil on which Gentiles walked as polluted.

The Essenes on their journeys are said by Josephus to have carried nothing with them, except that on account of robbers they bore arms.

7. he was much perplexed

Herod Antipas (son of Herod the Great and tetrarch of Galilee until he was banished in 39) has no compunction now in admitting responsibility for the death of John. Luke omits the graphic account of Mark about Herodias dancing (Mark 6).

10. the apostles . . . returned

It was a temporary campaign; the apostles' permanent commission in the Church will be bestowed during the Last Supper. Then Jesus leads them away to a quiet place, free from possible molestation by Herod.

THE FEEDING OF THE MULTITUDE

9.11-17

The reader of the Gospel could recall the miraculous feeding in a time of famine by Elisha in II Kings 4.42-44; perhaps also the feeding of the people by manna in Exodus. He could see too that the miracle looks forward to the Last Supper, and beyond that to the Church's Eucharist and beyond that again to the Messianic Banquet in the Kingdom.

The view of Schweitzer that the feeding was actually an eschatological sacrament and not a miracle is followed by V. Taylor, who writes: 'The multiplication of bread is a materialization of the tradition at a time when the true nature of the event had not unnaturally become obscure.' It is however unlikely that the feeding could have been thus misunderstood by a writer who is highly eschatological and who plainly gives it a Eucharistic, sacramental context. Surely it is more plausible to suppose that Mark had exactly the qualifications to understand very well.

The multitude may have been an armed rabble (Matt. 14.21 notes that though there were women and children the five thousand were all *men*) and were hoping to hear from Jesus a call to armed revolt under his leadership. Instead, these sheep without a shepherd are given a sign of his compassion, a sacrament which binds the whole company together in union with the Messiah who is to die.

In the Eucharistic symbolism of the early Church fish sometimes replace wine, but the fact that fish were never employed as the actual matter of the sacrament is a witness to the authenticity of the Gospels' description of the feeding. Had it been an invention of the Church, the story-makers could hardly have avoided making Jesus take bread and *wine*.

16. he took . . . he blessed . . . brake   gave

Cf. St. Paul's account of the Last Supper in I Cor. 11.23-26, and also John 6.11.

looking up to heaven

One ancient Eucharistic liturgy of the sixth century includes these words in its recital of the words of institution, and the gesture is still ordered to be made by the priest in the Roman Canon. Herod wonders who Jesus can be; then the feeding shows that he is the Bread of Life. The multitude does not believe. But of the disciples Peter at least believes and before long (35) Peter will have confirmation by the voice from the cloud.

17. The rabbis often warned people not to waste food. John 6.12-13 is more emphatic; this Bread feeds, yet (John 6.27) still 'abides'.

PETER'S CONFESSION AND THE TRANSFIGURATION

9.18-36

20. The Christ of God

Peter replies on behalf of the Twelve showing that, imperfect as their knowledge of Jesus may be, by contrast with the ignorance of the crowd they have been given an insight into the truth. The crowd accorded Jesus the title of prophet; but a prophet only prepared the way for something or someone greater. By revelation, the apostles, who have received the mystery of the Kingdom of God, confess Jesus' Messiahship.

Luke has added the word DAILY in 23 to Mark's uncompromising demand. This does not weaken it to a general instruction to self-discipline any more than St Paul's daily dying (I Cor. 15.31) is to be reduced to a mere metaphor for self-renunciation. Both Luke and Paul were thinking of persecutions and other ordeals of Christian witness.

24. his life (or **soul,** marg.); **true self** (NEB)

The life or soul is not a *part* of man, but man in his capacity of a living being with consciousness and will. Just as Adam once became a living soul (I Cor. 15.45) when God breathed into him the breath of life, so it continues to be true that the duration of life depends upon God and it may be lost, or forfeited, or cease to exist. Cf. Dr Faustus, to whom the devil promised everything he wanted, provided that in the end he gained his soul (to Mephistophiles):

> 'Go bear these tidings to great Lucifer . . .
> Say, he surrenders up to him his soul,
> So he will spare him four and twenty years,
> Letting him live in all voluptuousness;
> Having thee ever to attend on me,
> To give me whatsoever I demand. . . .'   (Marlowe)

27. the kingdom of God

Mark (9.1) records the saying in the form, ' . . . see the kingdom come in power' (NEB), which some interpret as 'see that the kingdom has (already) come in power' i.e. in the events of the life, death and resurrection of Jesus. Others have seen it as a prophecy of events that were fulfilled in AD 70, or in the Church's progress throughout the Empire. If however Mark 9.1 is a reference to the coming of the transcendent kingdom in its fulness, a visible manifestation of God displayed in the life of an elect community, then *either* the prophecy has not been fulfilled, and Jesus was mistaken in a most important matter of his teaching: *or,* the concept of the kingdom must be wide enough to embrace both the Messianic events in Jerusalem as well as the future comings of the Lord which the early Church experienced, and we still experience, in the sacraments, until the final coming. The latter view is what Luke tries to teach both in the Gospel and in the Acts, and to be clearer, he alters Mark. That generation would see the glory, but not the End.

28-36. *The Transfiguration*

Whereas the fourth evangelist demonstrates that the whole of the Lord's life, culminating in the 'hour' of his Passion and Resurrection, is a continuous revelation of the glory of God, the synoptists convey their understanding of Jesus' glory by means of the single incident of the Transfiguration and Jesus' teaching which it evokes.

There are two questions here. What happened on the mount? And, what was the probable significance of the Transfiguration for Luke? There has been a good deal of scepticism as to whether such an event could have taken place. The most plausible of the theories to account for it was to suppose that in origin the Transfiguration was one of the mystical experiences enjoyed by the disciples after the 'Resurrection' and which has been mistakenly transposed to the period of the ministry; though it is not quite clear why, after the Resurrection, Moses and Elijah should have been seen. But the decisive argument against this theory is provided by a comparison of the *form* of this story with that of the genuine post-resurrection stories. The latter invariably begin with the Lord absent; soon he arrives; and speaks; and so reveals himself. But in the Transfiguration account he is present throughout, and though he talks (30) to Moses and Elijah, no words are recorded and the silence is broken at the end by Peter.

If then the Transfiguration does belong to the time of the ministry, the next question is what happened. Was it just a mystical experience of one of the disciples who 'saw' the Lord in glory, as, say, Julian of Norwich saw 'three heavens'? But this is not necessarily so. It cannot be irrelevant that a similar radiance, transforming the whole bodily appearance, is recorded of some of the saints and other persons of sanctity. These cases of luminosity are not so well known as the stigmata which remained with St Francis of Assisi from the day of their appearing until his death or of Padre Pio in modern Italy, or the prolonged fastings of Theresa Neumann in modern Bavaria (see V. Sackville-West, *The Eagle and the Dove*). But they are well authenticated, and it is natural to suppose that the Lord's body also underwent either a paranormal or a supernatural change. The devout usually assume that all such phenomena are supernatural in character; the sceptical that they are all explicable in the light of modern psychological knowledge without recourse to the supernatural. Yet there is a third possibility: that certain of these remarkable events were supernatural graces bestowed by God upon his chosen servants and that others are imitative and merely unusual. And if the Transfiguration of Jesus had no natural cause, it is credible that similar radiance should be experienced by the saints, for 'the glory which thou hast given me I have given unto them' (John 17.22). The evangelists' description of Moses and Elijah was a means of expressing a truth about the unique Person of Christ. It was a way open to them of explaining, at this point, how Jesus fulfilled the OT; and Jesus himself thought of his mission on these lines.

What was the significance of the Transfiguration for Luke?

According to Exodus ch. 34 and I Kings ch. 19 Moses and Elijah both met the Lord God on a mount, and these OT encounters were in the minds of the evangelists. Moses had asked to see the glory of God, but the answer was given that no man shall see God and live; therefore God's glory was kept out of sight and for Moses' protection the Lord covered his eyes with his hand. Yet when he returned from his communion with God, his face had caught something of the divine glory, and, now for the protection of the people, he was obliged to put a veil over his face (34.33-35). At the Transfiguration however the glory is no mere reflection, but Messiah's own glory, such as will be for ever his after the Ascension—now, by a divine anticipation, seen to pour forth from him. He is of course the central figure, and to him Moses and Elijah bear witness; the former because he was expected by the Jews to have a rôle in the Messianic Age; and speculation about this was encouraged by the enigmatic note in Deut. 34.6 that 'no man knoweth of his sepulchre'. Elijah too who had been translated into heaven was expected to return to herald the Messiah. These two figures represent the Old Order; Jesus, the New Moses and Elijah, is to be the leader in a more wonderful exodus than that from Egypt and brings the work of both to fulfilment.

Jesus' RAIMENT became dazzling white (29). Clothes are intimately associated in the Bible with the person of the wearer. Thus in the NT there are references to the garment of salvation which the new Christian puts on at baptism, and to the 'new robe' of the elect. Here then the RAIMENT may stand for the personal and particular integuments of the Incarnation: they represent the mission of Jesus in human history in which and through which God glorifies the Son of Man. The cloud is a frequent symbol for the presence of the activity of God (Lev. 16.2; II Chron. 5.13, and especially Ex. 24.15): notwithstanding appearances, the presence of God rests upon the Son of Man. Jesus does not now remain in the cloud: this will happen at the Ascension, when he goes to be with the Father for ever.

The disciples slept and then were awakened. (This is to be preferred to the translation of RSV that they were only heavy with sleep and kept awake.) They slept—blind at first to the Messianic glory, deaf to his teaching that the glory of the Son involves the Cross (31). Then Peter babbles. But, since in the Jewish view God might dwell on earth in a 'tabernacle', his suggestion is not so much foolish as misconceived. It was a mistake to specify THREE TABERNACLES, for Moses and Elijah are not in the same category as the Lord; and this error is corrected by the heavenly voice when it affirms that Jesus is God's unique Son. But it was not really necessary to make any tabernacles at all for God to dwell among his people now. Peter certainly did not know what he was saying. For the flesh of Jesus was itself the tabernacle in which God was dwelling (cf. John 1.14: 'and the Word was made flesh, and tabernacled amongst us', RV marg.).

The divine VOICE, coming at the end of the scene, sets the seal of divine approval on Jesus, and because he is the fulfiller of the OT, Moses and Elijah can now disappear. On the mount the disciples beheld the Lord's glory, glory as of the only-begotten of the Father, a glimpse to them of the final glory that was to be, but a glory won through suffering and death (22, 26). This they hardly understood and again (44) Jesus must try to teach them about the conditions of his glory.

As with the Lord, so with the disciple (John 17.22; I Peter 5.1). The glory of Christ is present in the Church, which is the Temple of God, and we must share the glory of his Passion as well as the glory of his exaltation (II Cor. 12.10). The Church's prestige and political power therefore are not necessarily glorious, and while there is immense need in the Church militant for strong leadership, able preaching and genuine diplomacy, there is also a wrong sort of ecclesiastical success which is aggressive and statistical, too much occupied in public affairs just because they are public, too arrogant, and too confident about the ethical advantages of Christian belief. Whereas, if the Church were strictly loyal to her gospel of Transfiguration, of glory through suffering, 'we are bound to appear irrational, quixotic, futile, silly. If we do not appear so, it is because we have lowered the flag and are striving to fight the world with its own weapons—a course which nothing could redeem from insincerity save its inherent stupidity. For these children of the world are, in their generation, wiser

—very much wiser—than the children of light' (N. Figgis, *The Gospel and Human Needs*, 1909, p. 67).

In Western Christendom the feast of the Transfiguration has not been observed with the veneration lavishly accorded to it in the East, though the abortive Revised Prayer Book of the Church of England (1927-28) included a proper collect, epistle and gospel for it on August 6th, and other Anglican liturgies have followed suit. But in the East the Transfiguration is a key to its understanding of the humanity of Christ and there is a hymn: 'Thou wast transfigured on the mountain, O Christ our Lord, and the glory has so caught the wonder of Thy disciples, that when they see Thee crucified they will understand that Thy Passion is voluntary, and they will proclaim to the world that Thou art truly the Splendour of the Father.' The Eastern tradition never allows itself to think of the humanity of Christ in abstraction, i.e., apart from his Godhead, and it regards the Transfiguration as a revelation of the Trinity—the Father (the voice) and the Spirit (the cloud) and the Christ who was to conquer death.

28. about eight days after

Luke has altered 'after six days' (Matthew-Mark) to ABOUT EIGHT DAYS AFTER. It has been suggested that this was done to make the Transfiguration fall on the octave after the first prophecy of resurrection (27). The Resurrection (on the first day) is thus associated in a way early Christians would tend to do, with (on the next first day) Christ's glorification. But Luke must respect the historical facts and feels obliged to write ABOUT EIGHT DAYS (cf. 1.56).

31. his decease

Or 'departure': Greek, *exodus*—so making the comparison between Jesus with Moses, who led the Israelities out of Egypt into the promised land.

BACK TO THE PLAIN

9.37-45

The noisy scene below is a sad contrast to the glory on the mountain heights. Luke omits the detail given by Mark that the crowd was arguing with the disciples (Mark 9.14).

THE MAJESTY OF GOD was seen in the exorcism, but at this moment of success, Jesus utters another prediction of death, which the disciples again do not understand. The words AND IT WAS CONCEALED FROM THEM even suggest that this was in the divine providence. At any rate until after the Resurrection the disciples never realized that the death had been a clearly foreseen necessity.

THE DISCIPLES REBUKED

9.46-50

The action of taking a child was not intended as a direct lesson in humility, but was to urge the disciples to care for the 'weak things of the world' (I Cor. 1.27) rather than to compete for the pre-eminence. They must serve the lowly and the dependent, and in so doing they will be receiving Christ himself.

But that strange exorcist—could he be said to receive Jesus? Should he not be warned off until he come to a better mind and a sounder faith? But, no, our Lord replies: what little faith he has is genuine enough and is a basis for co-operation. This reply might suggest that the Church should not be excessively rigorous in its terms for infant baptism: even a very little faith in the parents will suffice. They must not be repelled.

THE JOURNEY TOWARDS
JERUSALEM BEGINS

9.51-62

51. And it came to pass, when the days were well-nigh come

Luke alone records this incident on the journey up to Jerusalem and his language, reminiscent of the Greek OT, indicates that Luke is now starting a section of his Gospel which he regarded as specially important and which, taken as a whole, is unparalleled by Matthew or Mark. Jesus is the prophet like unto Moses, of Jewish anticipation, a new Moses who makes intercession for the transgressors as Moses pleaded for the people: one greater than Elijah (19) or the new Elijah (7.27-28) who had prepared his way, going before the face of Jesus. The latter now in fact sends his own messengers (52) before his face.

that he should be received up

The same Greek word is used in the OT of Elijah's translation into heaven. But Luke may be thinking not only of Jesus' Ascension, but also of what preceded it. A work called the *Assumption of Moses*, which Luke probably knew, used the same word in connection with Moses' mysterious death and journey to heaven as well as the injunction he gave beforehand to his successor. Luke then is here thinking of Jesus' death and resurrection and Ascension, and regards this as the appropriate place for injunctions to his representatives who would rule in his Kingdom.

52. and sent messengers

When Moses was leading Israel towards the Promised

Land he sent out 'twelve men of you, one man for every tribe' (Deut. 1.23) to search the land; so Jesus likewise sends his disciples BEFORE HIS FACE.

53. they did not receive him

The inhospitable Samaritans are elsewhere portrayed by Luke in markedly sympathetic terms. But their unpleasantness here is exactly what might have been expected. The Samaritans were racially very mixed and in religion they were open to foreign influences that made for a very un-Jewish syncretism. They too looked for a Messiah; they too had a temple (on Mount Gerizim); but they only used the first five books of the OT. The hostility of orthodox Jews goes back to the time of Nehemiah and Ezra.

James and John are roundly castigated. Theologically, Jesus may fulfil (perfect) Elijah's work, but there is no imitation of the morally wanting ferocity of Elijah (II Kings 1.10); thus Jesus gives a concrete example of what he had taught at 6.29.

It would seem that while John the Baptist was generally regarded as the New Elijah who heralded the approach of Messiah, it was also possible to regard the Lord himself as the New Elijah. Jesus had himself made such a comparison when preaching at Nazareth (4.23-26), and there is a resemblance between what Jesus did at Nain (7.11-16) and what Elijah did at Zarephath (I Kings 17). In the present chapter the words of 51 echo Elijah's ascension (II Kings 2.1); and 52-56 are the proof that Luke intends to make the parallel. The Lord is the New Elijah; but whereas the OT prophet had brought down fire to destroy, the NT Elijah would send down the fire of the Holy Spirit to save (Luke 3.16; Acts 2.3, 4). And as Elisha was vested with his master's authority when he had gone, so the apostles are given Jesus' authority. Elisha helps Naaman, Peter helps Cornelius (both are Gentile soldiers). But the following verses (9.61-62) will show that the New Elijah

claims an allegiance and loyalty which far transcends even
that demanded by his OT predecessor.

57. I will follow thee

The group of would-be followers do not realize what
discipleship involves. The first is enthusiastic, but was
evidently not prepared for total lack of security with Jesus.
The second, eager to perform the proper Jewish duty
of burying his father, has to be told that even this claim
is secondary to the absolute claims of discipleship. The
third only asks to be able to do what Elisha did (I Kings
19.20); but family considerations too are secondary. A
ploughman who looks round will ruin the straightness of
his furrow! As Elisha was ploughing when Elijah called
him, this emphasizes that the demands of the Kingdom
exceed that of the Jewish Law.

58. hath not where to lay his head

As Jesus certainly had friends at whose houses he stayed,
the saying must be understood figuratively of his rejection
and sufferings. It is a warning to his would-be follower,
and means just what Jesus said at 9.23.

———

On this central section of the Gospel (9.51 to 18.14) see
p. 20. Luke is here concentrating teaching of Jesus into a
scheme of his own, and the journey to Jerusalem is an artificial, literary device. Jesus is no nearer the city at 18.31
than he is at the end of ch. 9.

X

SEVENTY ELDERS

10.1-20

Here the detailed parallels with Deuteronomy begin. Jesus
and the disciples travel from the Mount of Transfiguration
to Jerusalem, as Israel in Deuteronomy ch. 1 journeys from
Horeb to the borders of the Promised Land. And just as
Moses appointed twelve princes over the people (Numbers
1), and later seventy elders to assist in dealing with the
complaints of the mixed multitude, so Jesus first appointed
the twelve apostles; now seventy others are sent INTO EVERY
CITY AND PLACE, of the mixed races of the Galileans and
the Samaritans, where he was about to come. Later we
shall be told that the twelve will sit on thrones to judge
the tribes of Israel (22.30). The Seventy—on Jewish
reckoning there were seventy nations of the world (Gen.
10)—go out among the nations. The twelve princes are the
'type' of apostolate; the seventy elders are the 'type' of
the Christian presbyterate. By the time that Luke is writing, the original apostolate was nearly defunct and he
therefore feels able to recount the Lord's instructions to
them more briefly (9.1-6) than Mark. On the other hand
the elders, being the responsible officials of his own time,
are given much fuller treatment. But it was a fact of history
that the seventy appointed by our Lord were not a permanent and coherent body. While the ranks of the apostles
were brought up again to twelve by the election of Matthias
for the duty of bearing witness to the Risen Lord, the

Seventy fade into the unknown. Their disappearance is made good in the Acts. The twelve there use their authority to make Seven assistants (Acts 6) to replace the lost Seventy, and these deal with the complaints of the mixed race of Hellenists. They are the first presbyters (the word *deacons* is not mentioned), and do not share the authority of the apostles, who alone at that time have the direct and immediate authority of Christ. So in the Gospel it is the twelve who preach on behalf of Christ (9.2), while the Seventy have the subsidiary rôle of preparing for the forthcoming visits of the Messiah. In the Acts, again, Philip, one of the Seven, cannot do the apostles' work of bestowing the Holy Ghost with the authority of Christ, for only the apostles have that authority.

In the course of years, with the growth of the Church, more executive responsibilities devolved on the local elders, while apostles and apostolic men like Timothy and Titus watch over their scattered communities from a distance. There was a further development when one of the elders or presbyters in each local Church was given pastoral oversight and authority to exercise certain apostolic functions. The apostolate had been succeeded by the episcopate.

17. the seventy returned

They are full of their success, and report that devils were subject to them; Jesus sees in a vision the defeat of Satan falling as lightning falls from heaven. He bids the Seventy rejoice that their names are written in heaven. It is no surprise to read later (in the Acts) that one of the Seven, Stephen, wrought notable miracles, and that as he dies he knows that his name is WRITTEN IN HEAVEN.

JESUS REJOICES

10.21-24

In this section the language of Luke (with a few variations, also in Matthew) comes very near to that of John.
In ecstasy Jesus expresses his certain conviction of unique
sonship: his teaching has been directly revealed to him
by his Father.

22. to whomsoever the Son willeth to reveal him
The Son reveals the Father to the Church; but the meaning of NO ONE KNOWETH WHO THE SON IS, SAVE THE FATHER
is more obscure. It is perhaps a reference to the voice at
baptism which drew an absolute distinction between the
only Son and all other men in the course of the very act by
which he identified himself with them.

24. many prophets
This would include Isaiah and Jeremiah, while among the
KINGS would be David and Solomon.

ON LOVING OUR NEIGHBOUR
—AND GOD

10.25-42

25. lawyer
A man well versed in all the intricacies and interpreta-
tions of the Jewish Law. He TEMPTED Jesus, i.e. tried to
lure him into some unacceptable statement. Jesus replies
by getting him to quote Deut. 6.5 and Lev. 19.18: he had
known this law from childhood; he supposed that he
could practise it; supposed he could love God with all his
heart; supposed he could love his neighbour as himself!
There are many verbal parallels in this part of Luke to
Deut. 6 and 7.
With our knowledge of the delusions and stratagems of

the human psyche, we can guess that Jesus' reply, THIS DO, AND THOU SHALT LIVE, was gently ironic. He could *not* do it. Could he then live? But the lawyer instead of confessing his failure would JUSTIFY HIMSELF: how can you tell who your neighbour actually is? Jewish tradition confined one's neighbour to fellow-Jews, for example. The famous parable which follows does more than answer the question: it gives a practical example of the sort of way in which one can love one's neighbour.

JERICHO is 800 feet below sea-level, 17 miles N.E. of Jerusalem.

The PRIEST and the LEVITE, supposing the unconscious body to be a corpse, are not, by their own standards, callous and brutal. They wish to avoid ceremonial defilement, which they would incur if they were to touch a dead body, and they would forfeit their right to receive tithes.

OIL AND WINE were used in the temple sacrifices, and verse 34 must be regarded as a commentary on Hos. 6.6.

PENCE is a rendering of the Greek—originally Latin—*denarii*—the silver coins that circulated throughout the Roman Empire. One *denarius* was worth about sixteen *asses*, and bread and a pint of wine could be bought for one *as*.

38. a certain village

According to John, Martha and Mary lived at Bethany, but this would hardly suit Luke's itinerary. Luke here uses a piece of tradition, and calls it vaguely A CERTAIN VILLAGE, in order to fit into his scheme and correspond to Deut. 8.1-3: man does not live by bread alone, but by every word that comes forth from the mouth of God. Mary illustrates just this—while Martha occupies herself with the bread.

41-42. The Greek manuscripts have an air of uncertainty about Jesus' rebuke to Martha, and it would seem that Jesus simply said that only a few things were needed (see RV marg.): a warning against being too anxious and fussy.

XI

THE LORD'S PRAYER

11.1-4

There were certain prayers which Jews said as a matter of obligation, as well as their personal and private prayers. The disciples now ask for a suitable prayer which might be used by the little community corporately, as apparently the Baptist's disciples already did.

2. thy name

God's revelation of himself in history is to be received with the utmost reverence and this attitude must be given expression in the daily lives of Christians—for 'on earth as it is in heaven' which is found in some manuscripts at the end of this verse borrowed from Matt. 6.10, applies to this clause as well as the petition for the coming kingdom. The bread we pray for is the bread of the coming day of the Kingdom and the Eucharistic Bread wherein we anticipate the Day at the End. The temptations we ask to be spared ('Do not allow us to come . . .') are either temptations to sin, or the dreadful agonies which are the possible retribution of obdurate sinners, or the final trial—in an eschatological sense—at the End. Some manuscripts add the further petition, 'But deliver us from evil', and the Doxology which often concludes the Lord's Prayer ('For thine is the kingdom . . .') is given by a few manuscripts at the end of the version of Matthew 6; and it is also in the early Christian manual called the *Didache.*

A FATHER'S LOAVES AND FISHES

11.5-13

This Lucan parable gives a fascinating side-light on contemporary social conditions. Shops, such as existed in Roman towns, do not exist in Palestinian villages; otherwise no doubt the proprietor of one rather than a friend would have been disturbed at midnight. The family's bread was baked at the beginning of the day, but the primary duty of entertaining a visiting guest could not be ignored. The friend did not conceal his anger at being roused and shouted brusquely that the door has had its great bolt drawn and his whole family are in bed. 'We are to imagine a single-roomed peasant's house, on which the whole family slept on a mat in the raised part of the room' (Jeremias). Yet the rules of hospitality prevail with the friend too, and, however grudgingly, he cannot go on refusing the neighbour's request. No more will God reject the cry of those who earnestly call upon him; though Christian prayer must be qualified as the Lord's was (22.42), and the answer to such prayer may be in similar terms.

9. Ask

But it must be earnest. And then our heavenly Father will give us '. . . good things', according to Matthew, which Luke explains as THE HOLY SPIRIT, which is the Father's powerful gift after Jesus' exaltation into heaven. So later, in the Acts (1.14) the Church's earnest prayer will precede the descent of the Spirit at Pentecost; and through prayer with the laying on of hands the Spirit will be bestowed on the Samaritans (Acts 8.15). The Spirit's gifts included not only the spectacular gifts of foreign languages, which have been experienced from time to time since the apostles' time, e.g. among French Protestants hiding in the Cevennes after the revocation of the edict of Nantes, but also the gifts of love and toleration which make possible Christian fellowship, and the virtues which St Paul enumerates at Gal. 5.22.

BEELZEBUB

11.14-28

Jesus is accused of working his exorcisms by magic. Beelzebub was presumably a prince of demons, but neither of the two explanations of the name altogether fits this character. It is suggested that the name is either a form of Baal-zebub (II Kings 1.2) and means 'lord of flies', i.e. the god who drives away a plague of flies; or that it means 'lord of dung'.

19. your sons

Your disciples: let them answer the charge! The SONS might have asked in reply why their exorcisms were not equally signs of the working of God. It was a matter of interpretation. Jesus' were done with THE FINGER OF GOD; they made good his claim for himself; they were congruous with the other divine acts done by God's finger, creation (Ps. 8.3), exodus (Ex. 8.19) or the giving of the Covenant (Deut. 9.10). In the second of these instances the magicians, though also able to produce some plagues, confess that lice are beyond them. Moses however, works 'by the finger of God', and so 'the stews of creation have their way with Egypt' (Christopher Fry, *The Firstborn*).

24. The unclean spirit

These three isolated verses (24-26) come in another context in Matthew, and are possibly attached to 14-23 by

Luke to confirm what he has written there. The power of
evil can only be finally expelled by the kingdom of God.
When the demons were expelled, they were supposed to
wander about in the desert, and when they required refresh-
ment, they might return to their former subject—with seven
others (seven because this was the number of completeness
or perfection). Here was a combination of every conceiv-
able type of wickedness.

27. a certain woman out of the multitude

The incident recalls 8.19-21 in that Jesus makes use of
a reference to his relatives in order to put the truth about
relationships with God. How lucky Mary is to have such
a Son! Yes, but still more lucky are sincere believers in
the gospel!

A GREATER THAN SOLOMON

11.29-32

It is tempting to accept the suggestion that the sign to
be given to THIS GENERATION (29) should read John (the
Baptist), and that the correct reading has been corrupted
under the influence of the word JONAH in the next verses.
Yet 32 shows that JONAH makes good sense in 29 also. The
sign is to be the preaching (as with Jonah at Nineveh). In
the parallel passage in Matthew (12.38-40) Jonah is certainly the sign to this generation, only there it is his three
days' sojourn in the belly of the big fish (which of course
resembles Christ's three days in the darkness of the
sepulchre).

LIGHT

11.33-36

Luke has here attached two sayings which happen to have in common the word LIGHT to explain the preceding section. That generation was blind to the one greater than Jonah because their evil eye shut out the light. In 33 the lamp is the word of God, which is not to be concealed. In 34 the lamp is the eye which apprehends that word, which may be either the eye of faith (SINGLE means undistorted, or generous), or the defective eye of unbelief. The eyes of the Pharisees are blind (not generous, but 'lovers of money'; 16.14), in that they refuse to SEE THE LIGHT. Cf.: This Life's dim wonders of the soul
> Distorts the heavens from Pole to Pole
> And leads you to believe a lie
> When you see with, not thro' the Eye. (William Blake)

PHARISEES AND LAWYERS

11.37-54

The last section introduces Jesus' denunciations of the Pharisees. (Luke's coherent story is a skilful combination of some miscellaneous verses from Matthew 23.) Jesus' discourse is provoked by the Pharisees' complaint that Jesus had not washed before the meal. This was laid down in the interests not of hygiene but of religious reverence by the Tradition which supplemented the Old Testament. But doubtless, as with a weekly day of rest, the law of religion was of great benefit to private and social health.

39. the outside of the cup and of the platter

Outward observances, whereas Jesus calls for inward ALMS (41), i.e. a life of authentic conviction and congruous behaviour. In 44 Luke has altered Matthew's reference to the whitening of tombs before Passover, which are then fair without and foul within, and the point now becomes: just as you can walk over corpses without realizing it, so you can meet high-minded Pharisees without perceiving what goes on under the façade of respectability.

45. one of the lawyers answering

THE LAWYERS are blamed for the meticulous elaboration of the Law which was their professional occupation. They canonize THE PROPHETS when they are dead and can no longer disturb the hierarchy (48).

The entail of the whole rebellious history of Israel will fall upon this generation, for the coming of Messiah implies that the final reckoning is due—OF THIS GENERATION! Zechariah's murder is recorded in II Chron. 24.20-22 (the last book in the Hebrew Bible). Aramaic scholars suggest that the Greek words rendered THE KEY OF KNOWLEDGE is a misunderstanding of what Jesus probably said, which was, 'You have shut the Kingdom of God before men and removed the key'.

53. the scribes and the Pharisees began to press upon him

Luke again emphasizes the hostility which will lead to Jesus' arrest. On Pharisees, see 5.17 above. It was a general term for those who practised a strict Judaism. Not all Pharisees were scribes (=lawyers, 10.25), but the scribes (=lawyers, 10.25), but the scribes, who devoted themselves to the study and teaching of the Jewish Law, were normally Pharisees. It was a point of honour that scribes gave their teaching without fee, and they earned their living by a secular job. Some were members of the Sanhedrin.

XII

THREATENED WITNESSES

12.1-12

All the divine secrets are destined to be disclosed at the Last Day; but before that the halting and timid confessions of faith (9.20) of the disciples must become triumphant and public, even though they will bring persecution. But this is far preferable to disobedience to God who has power to cast us·into Gehenna.

5. hell
'Gehenna' (marg.), the name used sometimes for HELL, was the name of the place outside Jerusalem where rubbish was destroyed by a continuously burning fire.

10. him that blasphemeth against the Holy Spirit
It would be blasphemy against the Holy Spirit if believers were brought before the authorities to testify to Christ and then, rejecting the Spirit's help, denied their Lord. Therefore, to drive away the Holy Spirit is indeed the unforgivable sin, worse even than blasphemy against the Son of Man by unbelievers, for whom after all there is some excuse. The apostasy of Christians is less forgivable than the opposition of non-Christians: Luke has clearly adapted this saying (cf. Mark 3.29) to the situation of the Church he knows. It is a good example of the way he uses his sources; rather than reproduce Jesus' saying in a mechanical way, he allows the heavenly Lord of the Church to speak to a later generation.

A RICH FOOL

12.13-21

13. bid my brother divide the inheritance
It was common to appeal to a religious authority in a
dispute of this kind, and it still falls to the lot of bishops
in India, for example. See L. Newbigin, *A South India
Diary*, 1951, p. 70.

The Parable of the Rich Fool is one which only Luke
gives us. It is designed to teach the extreme foolishness
(the Bible's usual reproachful term for lack of belief) of
quarrelling about earthly possessions when the Kingdom
is at hand. The Rich Fool, forgetting God, makes his plans
without realizing that his life's end is at hand. It was sensible
to build large barns, but foolish to turn away from the most
important decision of all. Life is more than the possession
of barns.

ANXIETY

12.22-34

Anxiety is unavoidable to a human being of ordinary
sensitivity, and in some circumstances can become patho-
logical. There is the natural anxiety in the face of death
and the extinction of the body; there is the anxiety which
stems from guilt; the anxiety which is caused by a terrify-
ing sense of meaninglessness. Anxiety is the property of
man the sinner and therefore our Lord's demand for perfection carries with it a prohibition of anxiety. It is not
possible to practise this precept in literal obedience, for
only one who has submitted absolutely to the will of God
(31) shall be free from anxiety. Here and now we can only
recognize the ideal, set our course towards it, and pray for
forgiveness for failing to achieve it.

32. little flock
I.e. ' God's chosen people '.

33. Sell that ye have
Another of Jesus' hard sayings, which must be understood like the rest of his ethical teaching. Thieves could knock down the wall of a house and moths could ruin rugs and tapestries, and both kinds of destruction of treasure were common in the East.

THE NECESSITY OF VIGILANCE

12.35-48

Instructions to the disciples to be ready for the coming of the kingdom. Long clothes to be tucked up ready for vigorous action, and lamps alight (cf. the virgins of Matthew's parable, 25.1-13), expectant. But the Master they await comes not to be served, but to serve. As spoken by our Lord, this could have referred to his Passion and Exaltation, but it can rightly be understood by the Church of the Lord's second coming and of her obligation to be ready for it. 37b, however, taken in conjunction with 24.30 and the washing of the disciples' feet (John 13) refers to the Church's Eucharists.

42. Who then is the faithful and wise steward
This section is put by Matthew into his eschatological discourse in ch. 24, but Peter's intervention is given only in Luke. Peter makes a distinction between US (the apostles) and ALL (the Christian people as a whole), and the Lord's reply is that a steward set over the household pending the Master's final return must be especially faithful. The Lord's representatives must not abuse their authority. Verses 47 and 48 are also confined to Luke and may have become attached out of their historical context

because of Luke's writing parallel to Deuteronomy. The corresponding section in Deuteronomy (ch. 13) deals with the sin, which incurs the penalty of death, of a prophet who wilfully misleads.

FIRE ON THE EARTH

12.49-53

Jesus brings the FIRE of judgement, and 'would it were already kindled'. He approaches his crucifixion (BAPTISM) and wishes desperately that the ordeal was over. This Messiah will not inaugurate the reign of universal earthly peace; on the contrary, on account of the allegiance to him of some individuals, families will be split in two. The NT does not give a promise that there will ever be universal peace or universal belief this side of the Second Coming: only the promise that true belief will not perish from off the earth.

INTERPRETING THE TIME

12.54-59

The multitudes are well able to make elementary weather forecasts, but they fail to see in the events of their own time that 'now is the decisive hour'. They should be able to see for themselves what they ought to do. But the parables are a warning not only to the listeners in face of the first coming of Christ, but also to Christians in face of the second coming. Thus, just as in his conduct of life a prudent defendant agrees a settlement with the plaintiff before the action reaches the courts, so Christians should settle their affairs before the coming day of judgement.

54. the west

The direction of the Mediterranean. To *the south* lay the desert.

56. this time

The Greek word for *time* in the NT is usually *kairos*, which means the time of Messianic fulfilment, and another word, *chronos*, is used for the time which is measured on the clock. The *kairos* is therefore a moment of immense opportunity, to neglect which is disastrous (cf. II Cor. 6.2) and the activities of Jesus are signs of this *kairos*, which his contemporaries should have seen as the patent fulfilment of prophecy.

57-59. The background of this parable of reconciliation is the habit of taking a case from one court to another, higher, one. You may be taking your *adversary* (i.e. the defendant) before a civil court, but he may turn the tables on you by taking you to the procurator's official or Hellenistic judge. So Israel's cruelty, or at any rate, her insistence on the very letter of the law, might ultimately lead to her eternal condemnation by the heavenly Judge.

XIII

THE CRISIS OF ISRAEL

13.1-5

Jesus is not discussing a question of the Providence of God
—why certain suffer while others go immune. The fact that
Pilate killed some Galileans as they came bearing offerings
to the Temple and the fact that eighteen men were killed
when the tower of Siloam fell should be a warning to the
whole nation, which is as guilty as those few.

That Pilate behaved thus savagely with the Galileans
accords with what we know of the man from Josephus.
There was one occasion when he had his soldiers mingling
with an unsuspecting Jewish crowd in the capital, whom
they suddenly and brutally beat down with clubs.

THE PARABLE OF THE FIG-TREE

13.6-9

Israel was like a useless fruit-tree and it had just a short
breathing-space before the verdict of condemnation. The
fig-tree in the parable is not a common fig-tree that has
been left to take its chance in the open, but was in a VINE-
YARD being given special care—but also liable to special
disapproval if it was barren. Cf. Amos 3.2.

ISRAEL REJECTS THE SALVATION OFFERED

13.10-17

Jesus chooses a Sabbath day on which to release A DAUGHTER OF ABRAHAM who had for EIGHTEEN YEARS been possessed by a demon causing weakness. The parallel section of Deuteronomy deals with the release of Hebrew slaves and utters a warning against hardness of heart as the day of release draws near.

THE MIRACLE EXPLAINED AS A SIGN OF THE KINGDOM

13.18-21

This liberation is possible because the Kingdom, in however obscure a form, is being brought. In Dan. 4, the symbolism of a tree in which birds lodge used for Nebuchadnezzar and his great kingdom. So Luke may have in mind the entry of Gentiles into the Kingdom of God.

A PROPHECY OF ISRAEL'S REJECTION BY GOD

13.22-30

And if the Kingdom is obscure it is natural to wonder if those saved within it are very few in number and the Lord's answer, true to the prophetic tradition, implies that this is the case. But Gentiles (29) will be included, which explains why the Kingdom is like mustard seed or leaven. The Israelites may have been first in point of time, but this will secure them no advantage (30).

THE LORD'S DEATH WILL SEAL THIS REJECTION

13.31-35

The PHARISEES must be acting on Herod's behalf. But Jesus scornfully rejects the advice that he should avoid HEROD, who is dubbed a FOX either because this is an instance of his cunning, or (and this is a more frequent use of 'fox' in the rabbinic literature) because he is a 'worthless, insignificant man' (Creed). At any rate Jesus is not to be deterred from his work yet.

32. the third day I am perfected

The double reference to three days is both a statement of Jesus' immediate purpose as well as an allusion for Luke's readers to the necessity of the coming passion and resurrection. The cry of anguish over Jerusalem suggests that, though the synoptists do not record them, there must have been other visits of Jesus to the capital. Jesus predicts the desolation of the Temple (YOUR HOUSE) and says that the city will not see him (again?) until they sing Ps. 118 at the Passover. As a mere statement that Jesus would reach Jerusalem in time for the feast, this, after all the references to his proffered salvation through death, would be bathetic. As spoken, it might have been a prophecy of Messianic triumph through death; in its place here it may refer to the entry into the city (19.38) with its promise of triumph to come. It was a Jewish tradition that Ps. 118 would be sung at the time of the Messiah's coming.

XIV

A HOST REBUFFED

14.1-6

Again Jesus enjoys the hospitality of a Pharisee: and
again he asserts his authority over the Sabbath, since on
that day illness and disease could only be treated lawfully
when there was danger of death. The Aramaic of Jesus
should probably be translated, as by Moffatt, 'When an
ass or an ox has fallen into a well. . . .' According to the
Damascus Document (discovered in Cairo in 1896; parts
of it also more recently at Qumran), 'If an animal falls
into a pit or ditch, a man shall *not* raise it on the Sabbath'
(13.23). But there was a more humane view among some
of the rabbis, to which Jesus is able to appeal.

CLAIMS ON GOD MUST BE RENOUNCED

14.7-14

The parables are not to be taken as practical wisdom for
the affairs of this present life, or even as a lesson in
humility, but are a picture in terms of this life which demonstrates a truth about the Kingdom, namely that it
is God alone who sets people on the right hand or on the
left.

12. call not thy friends

Taken literally, this is a prohibition against showing hospitality to friends and relatives; but if it is an assertion of what the standards of the Kingdom are if they are put in terms of this world, then it is, amongst other things, a picturesque and provocative way of saying that perfect love is entirely selfless. If this blessed state is reserved for the kingdom of God, it can nevertheless be anticipated in quixotic and paradoxical fashion by Christian disciples here and now.

INVITATIONS IGNORED

14.15-24

'The guests at the Messianic banquet will therefore be very fortunate!' To which Jesus replies that the guests must have been genuinely eager to enter the Kingdom, and this parable relates the mournful excuses of guests who had wished to receive invitations, yet at the last moment, when as is usual in the East the servant arrived to repeat the invitation, declined. '*You* are like those guests who declined and insulted the host: hence the invitation to the beggars and the poor, the multitude which knoweth not the law, the Samaritans . . . the Gentiles.' (Read details in the Acts, Luke means.)

Deuteronomy ch. 20 deals with the grounds on which a Hebrew is exempted from military service, including recent marriage, and it closely parallels the rest of this chapter. But the disciples of Christ, by contrast, must be ready to go out whatever the cost.

THE COST OF DISCIPLESHIP

14.25-35

26. hateth

The disciple must do violence to all natural affections if these conflict with the claims of the Kingdom.

28. which of you, desiring to build a tower

The builder and the king are not allegorical symbols for Jesus, as though the meaning was that Jesus wants truly committed followers—or otherwise will abandon operations! The two tales are parables designed to provoke the hearers to self-examination (cf. 9.59 ff.) and hard thought: they must not be like a farmer who could not complete his buildings or a king who seriously underestimated the strength of the foe.

34. Salt . . . is good

The essence of discipleship is self-sacrifice, and just as there is no use in the home for salt without savour, so in the Church there is no place for professed disciples who do not follow the ideals of the Master. (But there *is* surely a place for those who are not yet ready to be fully committed disciples; see 9.50. The Church is bigger than a group of the spiritually privileged élite.)

XV

THE FATHER'S LOVE FOR THE LOST

15.1-end

Jesus first addresses two familiar parables to his opponents who accused him of receiving SINNERS, that is, people of immoral life, or Jews who had an employment which involved dishonesty, or perhaps pedlars, or even shepherds (which would add point to the first parable), or those who had dealings with Gentiles. The point of the parables lies in what they teach about the joy of God when the lost returns home. 'Since God's mercy is so infinite that his supreme joy is in forgiving, it follows that my mission as Saviour is to wrest his prey from Satan at whatever the cost.'

5. he layeth it on his shoulders

A shepherd was obliged to lay a lost sheep on his shoulder and carry it, for when a sheep strayed from the flock it would lie down and refuse to move.

7. I say unto you

Those who repent have recognized their desperate condition and can then receive God's gift of salvation. The *self*-righteous have not begun to see the need for repentance.

11. A certain man had two sons

The parallels with Deuteronomy continue. Deut. 21.15-22 deals with a man's rebellious son and with the rightful restoration of a brother's lost property which is found again.

The parable of the Prodigal Son is also addressed to Jews—to those critics of Jesus who appeared to doubt the boundless mercy of God towards the lost, and it concludes with an appeal to the critics who were invited to see themselves in the rôle of the Elder Brother, without love, and rather self-righteous. The parable might well have been drawn from real life in that both sons have received gifts of property from their father, for which legal arrangements were certainly possible.

13. the younger son gathered all together

The younger son, perhaps only about seventeen, goes off into the Dispersion (of Jewish *émigrés* among the Gentiles) wastes the money, gives up the practice of his religion and is soon near to starving. He would gladly (16) have eaten carob pods, but could not bring himself to do it. Upon his return home, his father RAN (which was most undignified for the head of the family) in his eagerness to welcome him back. The prodigal returned is then honoured with a ceremonial ROBE, a signet RING, indicating the bestowal of authority, and the luxury of SHOES. THE FATTED CALF would provide a meal for the entire household.

32. this thy brother

'This brother of yours', this child of God whom you Pharisees call a sinner.

The elder brother is challenged to forgive too and to share in the joy, but the parable is unable to say that he did.

The main point of the parable lies in the father rather than in the sons, and teaches the eagerness of God-in-Christ to reconcile men to himself.

XVI

THE PARABLE OF THE
UNJUST STEWARD

16.1-13

The story of this Lucan parable is straightforward enough
until verse 8. The steward is a rogue, perhaps not even a
fictitious rogue, but a local character whose behaviour had
roused his neighbours—who were now listening to Jesus—
to indignation. 'But', our Lord says in effect, 'you should
take the lesson to heart. The steward acted with acumen
and promptitude when he saw disaster overtaking him. He
had the good sense to do something in the emergency.
Now you are faced with a crisis of far more tremendous
importance. Are *you* going to act boldly? ' Naturally, Jesus
does not commend the steward's unscrupulousness. He
commends his vigour. 8a means that Jesus, not the
steward's lord, praised the dishonest steward for his clever-
ness, and there is no justification for HIS LORD (RV). Evidence from the Dead Sea scrolls suggests that 8b should
be rendered: 'for the sons of this world are wiser in their
society than the sons of light.' They are far more energetic
and adroit than Christians are in the Church!

It is possible that 9-13 were spoken in a different context but have been added by Luke to the parable either
because of the association of the word RECEIVE in 4 and 9
as well as the theme of money, or because the section is
required for the scheme of parallelism to Deuteronomy
ch. 23. As originally spoken, it may be an invitation to

publicans to perform charitable deeds with their money, so that God will receive them. As attached to the preceding verses, it gives the steward a commendation not so much for his audacity as for his wise use of money. Perhaps this was a lesson which teachers in the early Church wished to impress upon their hearers. They noticed the possibility of extracting further, though inconsistent, lessons from the parable, and so first 10-12, and then 13 have been added.

On the other hand, it must be recognized that such an interpretation of 9 ('Make good use of your wealth to win God's friendship') contradicts Jesus' other sayings about the immense dangers of wealth to true life, and the impossibility of earning God's favour, and it does not give a clear meaning to the words OF UNRIGHTEOUSNESS which here means money unlawfully gotten, not just any money. Another interpretation of 9 has therefore been suggested, that it is a piece of grim sarcasm. Jesus has urged promptitude—but, he adds, if you don't want to follow *me*, then collect your possessions together and expect a future reward elsewhere with the devil and *his* angels. It is either/or: on the one hand you may accept my offer of the Kingdom of God, or you may choose to be without the tiniest glimpse of God. 'This is a parable about the importance of decision. To be faced with the call of Christ is to be faced with a decision binding one for all eternity. If one has no wish to ensure one's future with Jesus, then it is worth using every crooked means to get into the devil's good books, for there are no other choices and no other chances' (G. Paul).

It is, however, possible to relieve the steward of the stigma of dishonesty altogether if, in accordance with contemporary custom, he had been lending his master's property and himself taking the interest. What in the emergency he perhaps elects to do is to forego these profits, and *his* master commends him for this prudence.

For a suggestion how 1-9 can be applied to himself by

the Christian pastor, see the remarkable book by Max
Thurian, *Confession* (ET 1958), p. 109.

THE PHARISEES AGAIN CRITICIZED

16.14-18

A further saying on money is appended, and then the
subject is left. 16 presents a saying of extreme difficulty,
which is made all the harder in view of its appearance in
a different form at Matt. 11.12. The probable Aramaic
original is said to permit of the last verb to be taken as
transitive: 'everyone oppresses it'. This agrees with
Matthew in denoting hostile action against the Kingdom
and does not mean that the crowds are trying to force their
way into the Kingdom. The old revelation of God came to
its end with the Baptist and with Jesus' preaching the
eschatological age of the Kingdom has begun to dawn. In
Jesus the salvation of God is at work; the new era is here.
And EVERY MAN practises violence against it, i.e. all the
scribes and Pharisees do; and perhaps Herod Antipas (who
had persecuted John, 3.19, joined the Pharisees against
Jesus, Mark 3.6, Luke 13.31 (?), and had divorced his wife
in order to marry Herodias, who was herself a divorcee).
Verse 17 is a bitter attack on the Pharisees: it were easier
for heaven and earth to pass away than for the Pharisees
to surrender one particle of their distorting tradition. The
TITTLES, or crowns (hence the TO FALL of RV) were adorn-
ments added by the scribes to certain Hebrew letters.

18. committeth adultery

Jesus' prohibition of remarriage after divorce is without
any reservations and contrasts with the laxity of one school
of Pharisees, but is, oddly, not made relevant by Luke to
a Gentile society in which either partner could divorce the
other, as in Mark 10.12.

LAZARUS' RESURRECTION WILL NOT CONVINCE THE JEWS

16.19-31

The teaching of this parable (the only one in which the chief character receives a name) is again on the impossibility of evading the judgement brought by the Kingdom, and it is a particular challenge to the well-to-do Sadducees, who do not accept a doctrine of resurrection. There was an Egyptian story about Setne, supposed father of the god Horus, at Memphis which ends: 'He who has been good on earth will be blessed in the kingdom of the dead, and he who has been evil will suffer in the kingdom of the dead.' That story may have travelled to Palestine and been used here by Jesus to point his own moral, which is that no sign, not even the greatest, would serve to convince those sceptics. The torments and other details of the parable are merely picturesque touches and are not intended to be a literal description of our state after death.

The unusual appearance in a parable of a named person makes it possible however that Luke knew of the raising of Lazarus (recorded in John 11). This at any rate is more probable than that John has invented a miracle on the basis of the Lucan parable.

21. the crumbs

The pieces of bread which were used by guests to clean their hands; they were discarded under the table.

22. ABRAHAM'S BOSOM

is the place for the departed in the intermediate state between death and resurrection and is also known as Paradise (23.43). According to II (4) Esd. 7. [85], [93], the righteous dead and the wicked dead could see each other.

Of course if Luke knew about the raising of Lazarus, recorded in John ch. 11, it would give piquancy to verse 31. One *had* risen from the dead and still they did not believe!

XVII
THE JOURNEY TO JERUSALEM CONTINUES
17.1-19

1. occasions of stumbling

Stumbling-blocks are causes of sin or unbelief. Though they are bound to come, that is no excuse for those who are in fact responsible for them.

5. Increase our faith

Feeling Jesus' demand for total forgiveness to be impracticable the disciples beg Jesus to give them more faith, and the Lord tells them that the kind of faith they should have is an absolute trust in God; and that this will reveal the glories of the Messianic age. Matthew and Mark read 'this hill' instead of THIS SYCAMINE TREE, which will be a reference to the Mount of Olives which the prophet (Zech. 14.4) said should be removed in the time of Messiah.

8. Make ready . . . and serve me

A slave who works in the field does not expect to return home and be waited on by his employer, or look for an expression of gratitude for merely doing what he was obliged to do. So disciples, however many of the commandments they fulfil, are servants of God with no *claim* upon his gratitude or mercy.

12. ten men that were lepers

Very like Mark's story in Mark 1 of the healing of the single leper; but in this case the story ends with the return and the thanks of the Samaritan one and the thoughtlessness of the Jewish nine. Leprosy in the Bible is not usually the appalling disease known by that name today. But this may be one of the exceptions, for the severe disease had been brought in from Egypt by Pompey's troops, and these ten men had something to unite them which was stronger than the instinct of racial segregation.

THE COMING OF THE KINGDOM
17.20-37

20. not with observation

You cannot watch—as astronomers watch the heavens—for the coming of the kingdom.

21. the kingdom of God is within you

Evidence from the papyri has fixed the much debated question of the meaning of the Greek translated WITHIN YOU or 'in the midst of you' (RSV), as 'within your grasp'.

22. The days will come

The Lord gives more teaching to the disciples about the coming of the Son of Man. It will be the subject of the wildest rumours, but disciples must be on their guard against them, never ceasing to be vigilant. Verse 25 is a clear statement of the Christian belief, and there is a similar piece of teaching by the Risen Lord in 24.26, 46. This third prediction of the Passion does not appear in Mark. THE DAYS (pl.) OF THE SON OF MAN are the days of Resurrection, Ascension and Parousia, perhaps also Transfiguration; i.e. days of Messianic glory.

26. And it came to pass in the days of Noah

Two OT examples of failure to be vigilant are, (a) the world before the flood, and (b) the citizens of Sodom. The Judgement Day will come as suddenly: how unwise to look back! LOT'S WIFE was turned to a pillar of salt—because she was so attached to her possessions that she could not help looking round to see what was happening to them. The Judgement is pictured as taking place at night, when people are asleep, but also, curiously, when women are grinding. The chapter ends with a shuddering reference to the Roman armies with their standards of EAGLES: they will swoop down on Jerusalem and destroy it; and this is the inevitable corollary of Calvary and the beginning of Judgement.

XVIII

TWO PARABLES ON PRAYER

18.1-14

Both parables are peculiar to Luke. They give guidance to
THEM (the disciples). The widow, too poor to bribe the
judge, approaches him with only one weapon with which
to fight her powerful opponent, a dogged persistence that
will wear the judge down until out of sheer desperation he
gives her justice. The moral of the parable is in 7: God
will also pass judgement in favour of us, for he listens
patiently when we cry to him day and night. The parables
teach both the necessity of persistence on our part and the
reality of God's mercy, for he is the God of the poor and
needy, and of publicans and sinners. The parables are
making these single points and do not imply that the
character of God resembles that of the Unjust Judge.

**8. when the Son of man cometh shall he find faith on the
earth?**
   Well, the Parousia is delayed to give men every chance to
be ready (21.24), even if some Christians chafe at the delay
(17.22).

10. Two men went up into the temple to pray
   The hour of prayer would be either in the morning at
nine or in the afternoon at three. The two men prayed, as
indeed the ancients also read, in an undertone, the Pharisee
doing so in a conspicuous position. The Pharisee confesses
his virtues which include voluntary fasts and voluntary

tithes, over and above what the Law enjoined. It was real self-denial. But the tax-collector, though conscious of being shunned by the religious, did not react with defiance, but instead admitted his unworthiness, did not venture even to lift his eyes upward, and remained at a distance. He smites his breast in despair and does not know where to turn in his dilemma; his conscience argues, 'You should give back those fraudulent profits on which you and yours live'. Yet it was he rather than the Pharisee who went away forgiven.

The parallels with Deuteronomy cease here. They have stretched as far as the end of the law of Deuteronomy in ch. 26.

INFANTS WELCOMED

18.15-17

In default of any explicit description in the NT of the baptism of infants, this passage has often been regarded as its implicit authorization. The lesson that Jesus was teaching by the rebuke was that the children were showing us how readily we must come to Jesus and to the Kingdom. But it was not long before the Church used the story to justify its baptismal practices, and it is even possible that, as the story was transmitted through the oral period, it influenced the wording of baptismal formulae.

RICHES A HINDRANCE

18.18-30

A man of some standing enquires what entering the Kingdom might mean in terms of personal conduct, and is taken to task by Jesus for lightly calling him GOOD. The

words of Jesus cannot be a disavowal of his sinlessness:
the Gospels would not make sense if Jesus did not claim
to be the incarnate righteousness of God. Rather, Jesus is
testing the genuineness of the man's professions. For, alas,
the rest of the story shows too clearly that he has not
understood, or at least that he was not prepared to follow
Jesus. Jesus does not question his premise, that the commandments of God are related to the Kingdom, but he
adds another counsel: in order to follow him, it is necessary for this ruler to renounce his worldly possessions and
hand them to the poor.

28. And Peter said

The disciples are surprised by Jesus' comment in 25, since
the rabbis of the time regarded poverty as an evil, but
Jesus replies that in the Kingdom standards are reversed.
Poverty is blessed (6.20). This encourages Peter to remind
the Lord that after all they had left their homes to follow
him. Jesus promises that all who have made the absolute
renunciation will be rewarded, not in the same kind of
assets, but certainly in this present life as well as in the
age to come.

THE FOURTH PREDICTION OF
THE PASSION

18.31-34

But still the twelve are blind. It is to Jerusalem that Jesus
must go in order to accomplish the new exodus; in Mark
this is the third prediction of the Passion. Luke alters
Mark's spelling (*Hierosolyma*) to Jerusalem, in order to
suggest the theological overtones of the geographical goal
of Jesus. Or so it seems from Luke's use of this spelling
elsewhere.

BLIND BARTIMAEUS MEETS ISRAEL'S SAVIOUR

18.35-43

But the eyes of the blind can be opened by Messiah, as the disciples would later know, and as we can know. The beggar calls out with a Messianic title specially applicable to a national hero, and just for that reason rarely used in the Gospels, because rarely used by Jesus. Even the crowd told the beggar to HOLD HIS PEACE. The blind man was in dire straits, but knew enough about Jesus to feel sure he would help; and he was not disappointed. When he was healed he FOLLOWED Jesus. It is Mark, however, who (a) gives the man's name (Bar-Timaeus), and (b), at Mark 10.52, points the significance for the evangelists of this miracle by saying that the man 'followed' Jesus 'in the way'. For 'the way' was the early Christians' abbreviation for 'the Christian way' (e.g. Acts 9.2). The miracle is therefore written in the Gospels to be an invitation to the readers to recognize their own desperate condition, since then Jesus would grant them insight into his salvation. And, that given, they must be up and active in Christian discipleship.

XIX

'A HEATHEN AND A PUBLICAN' RECEIVES HIS SAVIOUR

19.1-10

1. he entered and was passing through Jericho

ZACCHAEUS (the name is Jewish; it occurs in the books of Ezra and Nehemiah) is exceedingly anxious to see the prophet who was well-known as a friend of his despised class, and Jesus peremptorily asks hospitality from him. Jesus' attitude however evokes hostility from ALL (not only the Pharisees), no doubt because Zacchaeus was a prominent official, A CHIEF PUBLICAN (verse 2) and because Jericho, being on the principal road from Jerusalem to the east, afforded special opportunities for dishonesty. One wonders if the twelve had gone on in advance and ascertained who might give them hospitality (cf. 10.8). By offering it, SALVATION, in the person of the Saviour, came to his house; even if in fact a Jew, one to whom the Lord's ministry was addressed (for Luke, just as much as Matthew, confines the Lord's personal mission where it was confined historically, viz. to Israelites and near-Israelites), he was an outcast and Jesus' courageous action therefore indicates by his deeds that he sanctioned the Church's future mission to the Gentiles. Similarly, Luke's emphasis on Jesus' frequent contacts with Samaritans, who were less than fully Jews, is by way of claiming the Lord's approval for the story which Acts will unfold.

THE PARABLE OF THE POUNDS

19.11-27

11. they supposed that the kingdom of God was immediately to appear

As they drew near to the city, the disciples (cf. 18.34; Acts 1.6) supposed that God's kingdom of worldly dominion was to be established there and then. But on the contrary: Jesus is to go away and when he is gone his apostolic vicegerents must act with energy and skill on his behalf. The parable has features which would sound familiar to the listeners; for Archelaus, who had built a palace at Jericho, had to visit Rome after the death of his father Herod the Great (4 BC) in order to obtain confirmation of his heritage. The parable would read perfectly well without verses 14 and 27 and these may belong to a separate parable, (consisting of 12, 14, 15a, 27) which Luke has interwoven with the parable of the pounds, though it was indeed the case that Archelaus' request was opposed at Rome by a Jewish delegation (cf. 14). The parable is not an allegory—note the ten servants, not twelve—and the fierce treatment of the enemies in 27 is but another detail of the true-to-life story, not a hint of how Christ will mete out vengeance to the disobedient Jews at the Judgement; but the words, WHICH WOULD NOT THAT I SHOULD REIGN OVER THEM, are surely a hint of the coming Passion.

THE ENTRY INTO JERUSALEM

19.28-44

The entry into the capital is shown to fulfil the prophecy of Zech. 9.9; it is noted that Jesus is the first to ride on

the back of this animal, as later it will be recorded that
he was the first to be laid in that particular sepulchre. In
this account Jesus is acclaimed by his followers, whereas
in John the inhabitants come out from Jerusalem to meet
him (John 12.13). It is again possible that the disciples
had gone ahead to make arrangements and prepared a welcome. As the party came in sight of the south-east corner
of the city, they burst into praise. The Messiah is coming
to the city of David! The long journey is reaching its
climax. But the city will not know what is for its PEACE
(42) and will be razed to the ground; a prediction found
only in Luke, so that Luke only of the synoptists separates
the entry from the cleansing of the Temple.

42. now they are hid from thine eyes
  THE THINGS WHICH BELONG UNTO PEACE, i.e., the salvation which is offered, is not perceived. There is here a play ·
on Jeru-*salem* (=peace). Jesus foresees that the splendour
of the city will be brought low because the inhabitants have
refused to recognize what was necessary for her 'peace'.

IN THE TEMPLE

19.45-48

Luke's account of our Lord in the Temple differs from
Matthew and Mark. Luke alone records that Messiah
taught in the Temple, which Luke mentions because of his
theme of the importance of Jerusalem. On the other hand,
because in Luke the eschatological crisis is prolonged backwards into the infancy of Jesus and forwards into the
apostolic Church, the sense of crisis which stands out of
Mark at this point is reduced. Thus Luke has abbreviated
the account of the cleansing to the barest essentials: he
omits the word Hosanna (May God from Heaven save

Israel!) from 38 (cf. Matt. 21.9), the details of Mark 11.15b and 16, and the words 'for all the nations' in the quotation in Mark 11.17. In Mark Jesus expels the traders from the court of the Gentiles, since with Messiah's advent it must be shown that the Gentiles must have their proper access to God: Jesus' violent action, which is in the prophetic tradition of acted parables, is a sign that though his earthly mission is limited to Israel, yet this was only a question of temporary necessity and in principle Jesus wished his mission to be extended to all. So, if we only had Luke's account of the cleansing, it would be difficult to explain Jesus' unparalleled violence in the Temple. As it is, we are able to see how the evangelists use their material in different ways in order to transmit the same basic truths of the gospel. Luke has plenty of opportunity (with the Acts to follow) of showing how by the death of Jesus the Gentiles are admitted to the privileges of the new covenant (and see 13.30), but Matthew-Mark have associated an account of the cursing of the withered fig-tree to indicate the barrenness of Old Israel with the implication in the story of the Cleansing, of the substitution of the Gentiles. All the synoptists also bring out the close connection between the cleansing, when THE CHIEF PRIESTS AND THE SCRIBES (47) SOUGHT TO DESTROY Jesus, and the death of Jesus, which, we shall learn (22.20), effects the new covenant for all mankind.

XX

JESUS' AUTHORITY

20.1-8

In Matthew-Mark THESE THINGS (2) refers to the act of cleansing; in Luke to the teaching. But in either case the issue of AUTHORITY is fundamental. If Jesus had no Messianic authority his action approximated to blasphemy, and this of course is the opponents' conviction. But Jesus counters by posing to them the awkward question of the authority of John the Baptist, whose mission Jesus accepted as the God-given means of preparation for himself, and through whose baptism Jesus had been endowed with the Holy Spirit. Moreover, John was respected by the people. First let the critics face the issue which Jesus' precursor had put before them, then he will discuss his own claims with them. Indeed if the opponents could answer Jesus' question about John, they had in effect also the answer to their own question.

THE PARABLE OF THE WICKED HUSBANDMEN

20.9-19

This was obviously directed against the Temple hierarchy (19), the tenants of the vineyard, who had refused to yield the fruit to the rightful owner. These guardians of

Israel—the nation is symbolized by the vine—had made the Temple a den of thieves. At last they kill the owner's BELOVED SON! This is the last generation, and (16) they must pay now for the burden of accumulated guilt. There is a threat—how dreadful it was for those who boasted of being the Chosen People—that Israel will be deprived of her heritage in favour of others; and the very cause of Israel's rejection, the stone which the builders rejected, when he is raised from the dead, will become THE HEAD of the new humanity. This psalm 118 was one of the Messianic proof texts of the early Church, so that *the Stone* became one of the titles ascribed to our Lord. Luke adds a verse (18) to show that the same STONE is ' set for the falling . . . of many in Israel; and for a sign which is spoken against' (2.34). Many will stumble at the Christ: but to persist in calculated rebellion until the judgement is to have the Stone fall upon one.

THE JUST CLAIMS OF THE STATE

20.20-26

The question about the tribute money was extremely delicate. It is true that the Jews used the Roman coins in their business dealings, but it was a compromise with their principles of national freedom, and if Jesus should have seemed to accept Caesar's coins as perfectly legitimate, he would lose popular support, while if he openly rejected the claim of Caesar, he would invite Roman attention. Jesus accepts the rightfulness of Caesar's proper dominion and agrees that he must therein be obeyed, but he rejects of course Caesar's blasphemous claim to worship, and in fact when those claims were pressed and the State became demonic, the Church would be obliged to resist such pretensions (cf. Revelation), even if it meant martyrdom. It did not come to that for some years, and both St Paul (in Romans) and I Peter 2, in spite of a threat of persecution even then, call for obedience to the temporal authorities.

The fact that Jesus both repudiates Jewish nationalistic hopes of armed resistance to Rome and also refuses to exalt uncritically the Roman State comes out more by his deeds than in any particular sayings. He associated with both collaborationists and Zealots alike, and indeed selected some of the Twelve from among these mutually hostile groups.

Dr Oscar Cullmann has written: 'It is not the business of the disciple of Jesus to assume the initiative in abolishing the State as an institution. Rather he is to give the State what it needs for its existence. On the other hand, as soon as the State demands more than is necessary to its existence, as soon as it demands what is God's—thus transgressing its limits—the disciple of Jesus is relieved of all obligation to *this* requirement of a totalitarian State' (*The State in the New Testament*, 1957, p. 51).

RESURRECTION

20.27-40

The law of Deuteronomy (25.5-10), though probably not observed in the time of Jesus, lays an obligation upon brothers who dwell together to beget a son on behalf of any of their number who chances to die without an heir. 'Her husband's brother shall go in unto her, and take her to him to wife, and perform the duty of an husband's brother unto her.' The suggestion by the Sadducees was that this law excluded a belief in the Resurrection: no doubt it was a stock argument against their Pharisaic opponents (cf. Acts 23.8). Jesus is unambiguously on the side of the Pharisees (cf. Matt. 22.34), but appeals to a

passage in the OT which was common ground to them all.
If God still has a living relationship with the patriarchs,
then they must be living and not dead: there is no such
relationship between God and inanimate matter.

JESUS CONSOLIDATES HIS VICTORY
IN DEBATE

20.41-44

41. the Christ is David's Son

Psalm 110 is one of the most common of OT texts used
in the NT to attest the Messiahship of Jesus. He is both
descended from David and (he here teaches) more: he is
David's LORD; FOR DAVID HIMSELF (the supposed author of
the psalm) is proof that the Messiah is his Lord. Jesus
may here be teaching that his Messiahship does not depend
merely upon his genealogy, (given in 3.23-38), however
impeccable. 'Son of David' was a title he did not feel able
normally to use.

WARNING AGAINST SCRIBES

20.45-47

46. chief seats in the synagogues

These were placed in front of the ark which contained
the sacred rolls of the Law and the Prophets, and the
occupants faced the people. The scribes are accused of
ostentation, exaction, and hypocrisy.

XXI

A POOR WIDOW

21.1-4

By contrast with the scribes is this widow. People could hardly help seeing her, for THE TREASURY consisted of chests with apertures shaped like trumpets and they lay against the walls of the Court of the Women.

ON FALSE CHRISTS AND THE END

21.5-38

5. some
Presumably some of the disciples (20.45). They speak in admiration of Herod's temple which was in building throughout our Lord's life and Jesus predicts its utter destruction. This, the third Temple, only existed in its completed state from AD 64-70. The modern state of Israel has made no attempt to restore the Jewish Temple and its sacrificial system.

7. when therefore shall these things be?
The disciples would like to know of some SIGN which will show that this is going to take place, but Jesus does not mention such a sign until verse 20 and in the meantime warns the disciples against false claimants to Messiahship. I AM HE appears to be the blasphemous arrogation of the divine title. Cf. John 13.19.

8. The time

The Greek *kairos* means the decisive Messianic time, and is properly reserved for the TIME of Jesus of Nazareth. There will be revolutions (9), as in AD 66-70, the years of the terrible Jewish rebellion when the capital was besieged. Yet even this does not herald the end of the world. Verses 10-11 are concerned with this end: but BEFORE the portents there will be persecutions (12-19). 18 cannot mean that the Christians will all escape alive, but is rather a promise of ultimate safety in the only sense that ultimately matters.

19. Endurance will be rewarded in the age to come.

20. But when ye see Jerusalem compassed with armies

We come here to a specific historic prediction, though it too is certainly eschatological in the sense that for a Jew the destruction of the Temple would be counted among the events of the 'last days' and be a sign of the judgement of God, as was foreseen by the OT prophets (22). The details of these verses may be coloured by what actually happened in AD 70, but that the Church had received some such instruction as in 21 from the Lord cannot be denied in view of the well-authenticated flight sixty miles northeast (towards the invaders) to Pella of the Jewish Christians in the city. Readers of Luke would note at once the fulfilment of this part of Jesus' prophecy and feel reassured that the remainder was thus guaranteed.

23. upon the land

Palestine; but in 34-36, at the conclusion of the discourse when Jesus has reverted to the end of all things, the same Greek word must denote the earth. This is probably also true in 25 if 25-28 refer to the End, when THE TIMES OF THE GENTILES are FULFILLED (24b). It is not possible to be confident about this, but 24 *may* be equivalent to Mark

13.10 and Matt. 24.14, which Luke omits. When the gospel has been preached to all the Gentiles, then the End will come: until then it is delayed by God. (The Parousia will not come at the same time as the destruction of Jerusalem.) St Paul may be alluding to the same idea in Rom. 11.25 and in the much disputed II Thess. 2.6. THIS GENERATION (32) means here 'the human race', which will survive until the End without losing the tradition of Jesus' words.

34. suddenly

The emphasis is not on the immediacy of the End but on its suddenness, as in I Thess. 5.2. Jesus gives a warning to be ready for the last judgement, which will be universal in scope (35); it is not a warning against debauchery in the last days of Jerusalem.

This chapter reproduces a great deal of the Marcan Apocalypse (Mark 13) but with some significant alterations in addition to that in verse 20. Luke omits the reference to the shortening of the time (Mark 13.20); he omits the ignorance of the Son (Mark 13.32), which did not need to be included since in Luke the Parousia is clearly postponed to an indefinite future. (Cf. 4.15, 17, 18, replacing Mark 1.15.) In verse 8, Luke adds to Mark 13.6 a warning against those who preach that the End is at hand.

XXII

THE LAST SUPPER

22.1-38

The feast of unleavened bread was associated with the Passover but was not really part of it. The lambs were slain on the 14th of the month Nisan, while the feast of unleavened bread lasted for a week, beginning on Nisan 15.

3. Satan

Luke, like John 13.2, ascribes the plot against Jesus ultimately to the machinations of the prince of the power of evil.

8. make ready for us the passover

Unfortunately it is not possible to be certain what kind of a meal the Last Supper actually was—whether it was the Passover meal, as a reader would naturally infer from 8; or whether some of the events recorded would have been impossible at the Passover.

We can start with the certain fact that Jesus died on the Friday afternoon and that he ate the supper with his disciples on the previous night, *in which he was betrayed* (I Cor. 11.23—the earliest account in the NT of the Last Supper), though as the Jewish day was reckoned to start and finish at 6 p.m., the Thursday evening would have been regarded as the same day as the Friday afternoon. The problem has always been whether the Passover had begun

at 6 p.m. on Thursday Nisan 14/15, so that Jesus ate the
Passover meal and died during the feast, or whether he ate
the meal and died on the afternoon of Friday Nisan 14, at
the time when the lambs were being slaughtered in preparation for the feast. The Fourth Gospel seems to prefer
the second scheme, while the synoptists the former, though
they do contain items which cast suspicion on their choice.
For example, it is extraordinary that the Trial and the
death could take place during the feast, that Simon of
Cyrene should have been coming in from the country at a
time when journeys were normally suspended, that spices
could be prepared, and so on. And does not Mark himself
in 14.2 suggest that Jesus died before the feast? And Luke,
seeing that this is incompatible with the rest of the synoptic
chronology, omits it. It is true that all these difficulties can
be met one by one, but all together they are an impressive
testimony in favour of the Johannine dating; and this is
what most English commentators have held. In this case,
they have to decide what sort of a meal then the Last
Supper was, and they hold that it must have been either a
Kiddush, a religious meal held by devout Jews, celebrated
on this occasion in preparation for the Passover, or a
Haburah, a meal taken together by a group of friends on
special days, and which was now invested by Jesus with
a wholly new significance.

However, both these alternative suggestions have their
own difficulties and the closer one examines the Gospels
the more it does look as though the meal *was* a Passover.
There are a multitude of details which exactly fit in with
the Passover regulations. Thus Jesus made special
arrangements for celebrating the meal in the city of
Jerusalem; it was at night; it was taken by a group of
friends, who reclined, who ate bread during the meal, who
drank red wine; with a remembrance of the poor and with
songs of thanksgiving. Last of all, as custom decreed, they
made a journey within the limits of the city.

It might be thought that astronomy could very soon settle the issue and tell us whether in that year Nisan 15 was a Thursday or a Friday, but this it cannot do. For apart from the hazards of calculation caused by the Jewish practice of adding seven leap-months into the calendar for every 18 years in order to iron out the difference between the lunar and the solar years, there is the very practical objection that the beginning of each month was determined by two 'reliable witnesses' who were charged with the responsibility of catching a first sight of the new moon, and of course one misty night would alter the date! The modern discussion about the Last Supper has been a nice example of the process of NT scholarship as the advantages and difficulties of each view have been estimated. It required expert knowledge of Jewish literature and calendrical systems as well as a sensitiveness to the theological standpoints of the different Gospels.

Quite recently there have been hopes of a solution along a new line. There is evidence from the Qumran scrolls that there was an ancient Jewish calendar which had not been altogether forgotten. It seems to be referred to also in the book of Jubilees (c. 100 BC) and may have been known to some of the Christian Fathers. Now according to this ancient calendar the Last Supper, a Passover meal, could have taken place on the *Tuesday* evening; in the next three days there is ample time for the betrayal and the trial, while the crucifixion would have taken place on the Friday afternoon, which according to the official calendar was just before the Passover actually began. If this is accepted, then the four Gospels can be reconciled. The synoptists are right in regarding the Supper as a Passover meal and John is right in showing that Jesus, the true Lamb of God, died when the lambs were being slain. But how then explain the fact that the synoptists do suggest that the meal was on a Thursday? This could be attributed to the misunderstanding of the Church when it got out into the world of

Hellenistic Judaism which knew nothing of the old calendar. When such Christian converts heard of the Passover meal, they brought it as close as possible to the Passover they knew so as not to lose the paschal note. But the important conclusion is that we have two NT themes—the Last Supper was a Paschal Meal; the Lord upon the Cross was the true Paschal Lamb.

Luke has done what he can to make the impression of the Paschal Meal indisputable. For this reason, the longer text (as in RV) at 19, 20 is to be preferred to the shorter (RSV). The longer has vastly better authority in the Greek manuscripts, but some scholars have suspected some of the scribes who copied the manuscripts of deliberately introducing the extra words in 19, 20 because they knew them so well from their own worship, in which I Cor. 11.25 was always repeated. It is however more likely that the alteration was the other way round; the shorter is a deliberate abbreviation, and that what happened was this: a few Christian scribes could not understand why Luke should mention two cups (17, 20), which is perfectly usual for a Passover Meal, but not in the Christian Eucharist. Therefore some unintelligent scribes left out the reference to the second cup.

Now for the theological question. In the Fourth Gospel Christ is presented as the true Passover lamb who dies to take away the sins of the world. Moreover, in view of what takes place at the other Passover feasts which occur in John, the idea is of the perfect sacrifice of Christ, embracing the whole of his life and consummated on the Cross. In the synoptists, the Lord and his disciples celebrate a Passover meal in which they looked both to the past and to the future: they recalled the deliverance from Egypt through the atoning power of blood and they regarded the rite as a pledge of the future consummation in the Kingdom. The Lord however takes the place of the lamb. The exodus from Egypt is replaced by the Exodus from the bondage of sin. His blood preserves us from the angel of death. And the Supper is to be repeated until Christ comes again, while by the words *This is my Body. . . . This is my Blood* he meant, not that these material things signify the Lord's Presence, but that they cannot be separated from it: the being of Christ really is communicated through the media of these material things and by them the believer is ever and again incorporated into the death and resurrection of the Lord. This is the *new* covenant. And when he says that this is his last Passover (15 f.) until it is fulfilled in the Kingdom, he is referring to his future presence at the Church's Eucharists, when he is 'remembered', i.e. brought back. Probably the apostles understood by such words the restoration of Israel (cf. Acts 1.6) but after the Resurrection Jesus appears to them and ate with them (Luke 24.30, 41-43) to show that under the paradoxical form of the Church his Kingdom was already present. He accustoms them to the notion of his Eucharistic presence; then disappears when he is recognized.

It ought not to be possible therefore for the Church to minimize the glory of the Eucharist, and yet this has happened in the Roman and in the non-Roman Churches. In the former, communion, which is part of the sacrifice, has sometimes been infrequent, and the Mass has been treated as though it were a gorgeous pageant. In the latter there has been that stifling tradition of Protestantism abroad according to which the Revelation is conveyed to men only in words, and in England a decline of sacramental practice in the Free Churches through fear of ritualism. But everywhere there is, at last, an impressive revival. The modern Parish Communion tries to reproduce both the solemnity and the corporate character of the Last Supper. In the Roman Church there is everywhere a wider participation of the laity in the Mass and a sustained attempt to understand what in terms of contemporary cultural patterns the Church's work actually is, while Protestant Churches have produced new liturgies, an enriched sacramental theology and new disciplines in community.[1] Writing in favour of weekly communion, a British Methodist urges the strong claims of a practice found in the NT, commended by the Reformers and practised by the Wesleys.[2]

29. A kingdom

Jesus promises twelve thrones (the election of Matthias is foreshadowed) to judge the New Israel (the Church), but the apostles must first continue with Christ in his ordeals (28). The twelve are given authority to rule the Church, and to preside at the Eucharist (30). Within the Church the future position of Peter as head is indicated by Luke though not in the same way as Matthew ('Thou art Peter, and upon this rock', 16.18). Satan has demanded *all* (YOU is plural in 31), but it is Peter alone for whom Jesus here prays and Peter is to strengthen the rest. True, Peter's boast was to come to nothing when the test came very soon, but in fact Peter was chosen by God, and readers of the Acts would know how he atoned for his lapse. They might also be aware of his courageous death at Rome under Nero (a tradition confirmed by recent archaeological discoveries at the Vatican, even if the site of the martyred Peter's resting-place remains uncertain).

It has been pointed out that there were really thirteen tribes in Israel. 'It is a singular fact that "Levi" [the priestly tribe] "and the Twelve" [lay tribes] is a form of reckoning in the OT' (Farrer, *St Matthew and St Mark*, p. 37). Nor in their insistence upon the parallel between apostles and tribes are the evangelists embarrassed by this OT quirk. If reminded of it, they will reply that there was

---

[1] See e.g., Max Thurian's *The Eucharistic Memorial*, ET 1961, F. J. Leenhardt's *This is my body* (ET in *Essays on the Lord's Supper*, Cullmann and Leenhardt, 1958) and G. Aulén's *Eucharist and Sacrifice*, ET 1958.

[2] A. R. George, in *The Doctrine of the Church*, 1964, p. 143.

Levi who was called (Luke 5.27) but not named in the list
of the twelve in 6.14 ff.

36. now

New instructions are necessary for the eleven, when
Satan is about to strike, including the acquisition of A
SWORD. Does Jesus contemplate for a moment an armed
resistance? Hardly; either the sword merely symbolized
the need for perpetual vigilance, or else it was part of the
deliberate fulfilment of scripture, for which a mere token
of TWO SWORDS is sufficient (38). The OT passage referred
to in 37 is Isa. 53.12 and is the only certain quotation of it
in the Gospels, though it was in general use by the early
Church to explain the mission of her Saviour.

Boniface VIII found the TWO SWORDS a convenient
justification for his views on the two authorities, worldly
and spiritual, of the papacy.

THE AGONY AND THE ARREST

22.39-53

Luke does not mention the name Gethsemane, as do the
other Gospels and which according to tradition was situated
just to the east of the Kidron valley, with the Mount of
Olives rising up to the east. Jesus bids the disciples pray
that they may not enter into the fiery trial. Luke alone
stresses the distance between Jesus and the disciples (who
are not mentioned in Luke by name) and alone condones
them with the words FOR SORROW (45). It is probable that
in some circles, e.g. in Alexandria after the triumph of
Athanasius, verses 43-44 were suspected of being inconsistent with the orthodox view of Christ's divinity. Some
scribes therefore deliberately omitted them. This at any
rate seems a more likely explanation of the textual vari-

ants at this point than that Luke never wrote these words
and that some scribes put them in.

The CUP (42) as Mark 10.38 shows, is a symbol for
death.

In Luke's account Jesus frustrates Judas' attempt to kiss
him, and, as he confronts the traitor, the disciples want to
use force. In Matthew-Mark they use force by way of
retaliation after Jesus has been seized. There is thus in
Luke a slight shift in a detail to emphasize perhaps the
majesty of Christ. So too in this Gospel the rulers come
out against Jesus, whereas in Matt. 26.47, 55, only their
servants effect the arrest. The POWER OF DARKNESS occurs
only in Luke. How it resembles John (e.g. John 13.30)!

AT THE HIGH PRIEST'S

22.54-71

Peter is challenged by three people in turn and then the
cock crows. The unforgettable note of the Lord looking
upon Peter is preserved only in Luke; it provokes the beginning of Peter's repentance.

The Sanhedrin could meet as a judicial body but could
not itself inflict the death penalty (John 18.31). It appears
that at this enquiry the high priest was able with some skill
to unite the several elements in the Sanhedrin by proving
that Jesus was guilty of what was in Jewish eyes a capital
crime, i.e. blasphemy against the Temple (Matt. 26.61).
Then the high priest enquired about Jesus' Messianic
claims (Luke 22.70) and, suitably worded, this formed a
charge (23.3) which could not be ignored by Pilate.

Jesus does not maintain a silence, as in the Marcan narrative.

64. NEB translation of Mark 14.65 shows that according to the best Greek texts Luke is here following Matthew (26.28), in preference to Mark (14.65).

67-68. These verses are closely paralleled by John 10.24-25.

68. if I ask you
If I put to you questions in self-defence.

69. from henceforth
After the passion and death, Jesus will enter into his glorification: through apparent defeat comes the certain triumph of the Resurrection and Ascension.

Jesus' apparently ambiguous reply, YE SAY THAT I AM, must be regarded as an admission of the title, but in view of the prosecutor's unbelief he affirms it with reserve.

Luke has conflated Mark's account of *two* trials before the Sanhedrin (Mark 14.53; 15.1) at night and next morning, into one trial at dawn (Luke 22.66), and thus made a more orderly narrative, though not necessarily a more accurate one (A. N. Sherwin-White, *Roman Society and Roman Law in the New Testament,* 1963, p. 45).

XXIII

In the Passion narrative the most interesting Lucan variation is the account in 6-12 of a trial before Herod; but this
Gospel is also noteworthy for its reiteration of the inno-
cence of Jesus and for its pains to exculpate the Roman
authorities.

THE RULERS TAKE COUNSEL
TOGETHER

23.1-25

Of the 162 words in the Greek of this section, a mere 30
occur also in Mark, which strongly suggests that Luke is
here using an alternative source of information.

It has been doubted whether Jesus could really have
been sent before Herod in the area of Pilate's own juris-
diction and suggested that Luke was determined to show
somehow or other that Jesus was found innocent by both
Jewish and Roman authorities; yet elsewhere in the
Gospel there is, to say the least, no effort to deny the Jews
their blame for the death of Jesus. It is their leaders who
bring him before Pilate and who demand the release of
Barabbas. It is also true that Luke probably thought his
narrative showed the fulfilment of Ps. 2.1, 2, but this does
not mean that he invented the story. From 8.3 it appears
that Luke was for some reason interested in Herod. The
trial may have been strictly illegal, but this was not likely
to worry Pilate, who knew that the niceties of procedure
in remote Judaea were of no concern to Rome.

Herod turns to contempt for Jesus; his soldiers carry

out the cruel mocking which in Matthew-Mark is attributed
to the Roman soldiery. Invested with a GORGEOUS robe
(Luke avoids the word ' purple ', with its regal associations),
he returns to Pilate, who seems to suspect that the charge
is in some way irregular. But under pressure he releases
Barabbas and condemns Jesus. There is evidence from
some manuscripts at Matt. 27.16 that the name was actually
Jesus Bar-Abbas, but not unnaturally Bar-Abbas' first
name (which was not uncommon among the Jews) dropped
out in the course of copying manuscripts by Christian
scribes: it was felt unbearable to allow him the same name
as our Lord himself. NEB reads, ' Jesus Barabbas '.

Apart from the Gospels there is no definite knowledge of
this custom of releasing a prisoner at the Passover, but
cases are recorded by Livy and the younger Pliny of acts
of clemency at the time of some local celebration, and
there is no need to deny the historicity of the event. At the
same time no doubt the early Christians observed that
' Son of the Father' was an apt name in the circumstances.
Saved by the vicarious death of Christ, Bar-Abbas was
like all of us who are sons of our Father in heaven.

THE CRUCIFIXION

23.26-56

The transverse beam of the cross was carried in proces-
sion as a deterrent to other criminals. Luke alone records
the presence of women among the mourners accompanying
Jesus and his lament over Jerusalem. In their agony of
heart, Jesus predicts, the mothers living in the city will
shriek the words of Hosea 10.8, praying that the moun-
tains will cover them. THEY (31) are the Romans; THE
GREEN TREE represents Jesus. So (Dr Cullmann suggests)
the whole sentence means: ' If they execute me for pretensions to kingship, who am no Zealot and have in fact

uttered warnings against Jewish nationalism, what will they do in the days to come to the genuine Zealot rebels? '

34. Father, forgive them

Luke alone records Jesus' prayer that the executioners may be forgiven. The fact that one or two manuscripts omit the words has led to the suspicion that the majority which possess them have been influenced by the same cry uttered by St Stephen (Acts 7.60), as though the Lord should be made to do no less than the first Christian martyr. Equally, however, it is possible that certain scribes deliberately omitted the words here, though they were in the versions they were supposed to be copying, out of anti-Semitism.

43. in Paradise

PARADISE is the transliteration of the Greek word (originally Persian) which means a park and which is used of course in the Greek OT in the early chapters of Genesis. In later Jewish literature the name was applied to that section of Sheol where the righteous departed live (also called Abraham's Bosom) and was held to be a place of repose, separated by an impassable gulf from the other part of Sheol, where the wicked suffer.

In Rev. 2.7 'Paradise' denotes the state of blessedness at the End and is an eschatological concept. If that were the meaning here, then our Lord is saying that TODAY, while he is apparently so weak, hanging from the cross, he is nevertheless reigning and can distribute death or life. But the former interpretation is more probable: the thief is the first to enter the abode of the dead since the death of Christ has altered its terms.

44. the sixth hour

The middle of the day; according to Mark (15.25), which Matthew and Luke do not follow, Jesus was on the cross from 9 a.m. John 19.14 has Jesus still before Pilate at mid-day. Such details cannot be reconciled.

45. the sun's light failing

The Greek words imply an eclipse of the sun, and the Church's enemies were soon suggesting that this is all it was. With some relish, Christian apologists replied that an eclipse was an impossible natural event at the time of the full moon. Luke may be thinking of a heavenly portent such as had been foretold in 21.25, and Amos had pro-phesied that there would be darkness on the Last Day (Amos 5.18). Early Fathers regarded the event as the fulfil-ment of words about the sunset in Ps. 104.19. And former pagans would see the event as more than merely natural. Cf 1.78.

Luke means that here God is indeed at work. The tearing of the Temple veil in two likewise signifies that we are in the presence of the mighty acts of God. (This veil probably divided off the Holy Place from the Holy of Holies, and through it the priest passed once a year on the day of atonement.) This incident may be 'a legendary addition doctrinal in origin', but it must be understood in the same way as the rending of the heavens at the baptism of Jesus. The latter indicates to the reader that in Jesus God had come down to earth, while the tearing of the veil describes the atonement now made between man and God. But whereas Mark places the tearing after Jesus' death, in Luke the verse comes *before* Jesus' last words (words which are in Luke a cry of trust and obedience to God). Luke is re-interpreting the tradition. In the light of the history of the Church, he does not wish to tie the testimony of both Jews (given by the Temple) and Gentiles (through the centurion) exclusively to the *death* of Jesus. Therefore while in Matthew-Mark the centurion confesses that Jesus was cer-tainly Son of God—historically perhaps no more than an assertion that Jesus was a son of God, one noble enough to have in him a spark of divinity, though for Matthew and Mark the first declaration of Christian faith by a Gentile—in Luke the centurion exclaims that Jesus must be *innocent*, or perhaps ' the Righteous One ', as the Jewish Christians thought of Jesus (Acts 3.14).

Zechariah 9-14 was a section of the OT much used by the writers of the NT to illustrate the truth of the facts of the Gospel, and 48 may have in mind Zech. 12.10-14, where the inhabitants of Jerusalem ' shall look on him whom they have pierced ' (quoted by John 19.37), and mourn for him, women separately from the men, as for an only son.

50. a man named Joseph

Instead of being allowed to hang lifeless on the cross, as usually with the victims of that barbarous torture, a member of the Sanhedrin or of one of the local councils of twenty-three members each (who had not agreed to the charge against Jesus, and who comes upon the scene at the end of the Gospel rather as do Simeon and Anna at the beginning) uses his good offices to secure the burial of Jesus in a virgin tomb. The burial was done in haste, without embalming the corpse, since the Sabbath began at 6 p.m. and there was little enough time to get spices ready before the compulsory rest started.

The evangelists mention Joseph's name because in the OT Joseph the patriarch had begged Pharaoh to let him bury Jacob (also called Israel). Now the one faithful Israelite is buried by another Joseph.

XXIV

EASTER

24.1-12

The women come at early dawn. They do not *see* the Resurrection, which is nowhere described in the NT. They do find evidences of the Resurrection—the stone rolled away, the body gone, and two men in dazzling apparel reminiscent of Moses and Elijah on the Mount of Transfiguration who had then foretold the exodus which Jesus would accomplish at Jerusalem.

6. when he was yet in Galilee

Luke has rewritten Mark 14.28 that Jesus will precede the disciples in Galilee and there manifest himself to them. Luke uses the word GALILEE but he rewrites the sentence both because he is not going to mention any appearances of Jesus there and because Mark 14.28 could have been taken as a promise of an imminent Parousia.

11. idle talk

They at first DISBELIEVED not because the notion of resurrection as such was incredible, but because their knowledge of the OT and the teaching of the rabbis would have led them to expect a corporate resurrection, a resurrection of the whole community. They could not accept the idea of the rising again in history of a single individual. They believed when it was *revealed*; the Risen Lord could not be recognized until he revealed himself (24.16).

12. Peter arose, and ran unto the tomb

RSV and NEB omit this verse, which is absent from some manuscripts. But it seems to be assumed by verse 24.

EMMAUS

24.13-49

The two know of Peter's visit to the tomb: can the un-named disciple have been Peter? Two of the early Fathers thought so. Verse 34 could easily mean that the two, not the apostles, said that the Lord had appeared to Peter. And hence the terror mentioned in 37: they had still to be convinced of the Resurrection. The obvious difficulty that in 33 the two go back to the 'eleven' can be met. It was the number to indicate the apostolic body even if one was missing, just as St Paul in I Cor. 15.5 writes of the Twelve when he means eleven! Another tradition is that the companion of Cleopas was James the Lord's brother (hence I Cor. 15.7).

13. Emmaus

Probably the modern Kulonieh, which is nearly four miles from Jerusalem in the direction of Joppa.

16. their eyes were holden

They saw with their eyes, yet did not 'perceive' the stranger, like Elisha's servant at Dothan who saw the mountain but not, at first, that it was full of horses and chariots of fire (II Kings 6.17).

21. he which should redeem Israel

They had been hoping even to the last that Jesus might bring off a political coup and establish an independent state. The second part of the verse again calls attention to the fact that it was the third day, the same day as that of the visit of the women to the tomb. The immediate observance by the Church of Sunday is the strongest proof of the authenticity of the experiences on the third day, but the Church was quick also to note the OT passages which gave support to the idea, such as Hosea 6.2. It is true that Hosea was speaking of the revival of the nation, but the Lord had identified himself with his people and suffered vicariously as the faithful remnant of Israel, so that his resurrection is in a true sense also the resurrection of Israel. Because he died, all have died: in that he rose, we rise too.

Vicarious suffering therefore means not suffering instead of mankind, but suffering *on behalf* of mankind, in that by incorporation with him all Christians have in a mysterious way died in the person of Christ. Yet because of the Resurrection of Christ, his death, and our deaths are not a defeat. 'Christians have died in, with and through the crucified body of the Lord (have a share, that is, in the actual death that He died unto sin historically), "once for all" (Rom. 6.10, RV marg.) because, and only because, they are now in and of His body in the "life that he liveth unto God", viz., the body of the Church' (J. A. T. Robinson, *The Body*, 1952, p. 47).

26. Behoved it not
It was *necessary* because only so could Christ enter into glory. This is also the teaching of John 12.32.

28. he made as though he would go further
But they begged him to stay and in the breaking of the bread the stranger's identity is disclosed (cf. John 21.9 ff.). And at once he vanishes. When fellowship with him is re-established, there is no need for the bodily appearance to remain. He had revealed to the disciples the true signifi-

cance of his own life and death which, without revelation,
they would never have perceived. Even while the two disciples describe the appearance to Simon, the Risen Lord
comes through the closed door and rebukes their unbelief;
he invites them to touch him and prove for themselves that
he is really there. He is no ghost, no angel; he can take
and consume a piece of fish (contrast Tobit 12.16-22). He
again appeals to the OT scriptures and shows that so far
from being an unheralded disaster, the crucifixion, and its
reversal on the third day, could all be found predicted in
the OT.

37. The prophecy of Ezek. 37.5-6 is fulfilled in a better way
than the prophet had imagined: Jesus is the first-fruits of
the New Israel.

42. a piece of a broiled fish
A few manuscripts make an addition here, according
which Jesus took not only FISH but also honey—plainly
an intrusion on the part of some scribes who guessed that
Jesus probably did the same as the Church when it had
admitted by baptism its newly-born children into the
Promised Land.

47. beginning from Jerusalem
Luke is careful to mention JERUSALEM once again, the
city of revelation, the city from which the good news will
go out in ever widening circles until it reaches the capital
of the empire. The most literary of the Gospels ends like
so many of the NT books (cf. Mark 16.8; John 21.25)
without a polished conclusion. Like the other Gospels, it
looks forward, but unlike them Luke is able to continue
his work with an account of Jesus' works in his Church.
But then Acts itself ends in a curiously lame way: even
that does not complete the story.

Additional note on the Resurrection

The concept of death and resurrection was familiar enough in ancient religions; Osiris and Tammuz and Attis died and rose each year. Such religious ideas of the Canaanites were not without their influence on Israel, but they were purified by the prophets into the idea of the restoration of the moribund nation by the power of Yahweh (Ezekiel 37) or, later still, into the idea of the resurrection of faithful Israelites who would be raised together after a judgement. (Luke 20.27 and Acts 23.6-8 are corroborated by Josephus in noting that this development was not accepted by the Sadducees.) These intimations of the death and resurrection pattern are natural if, as the NT asserts, the creation was made through Christ; the universe thus bears something in its make-up of the eternal obedience of the Son to the Father which was uniquely expressed at a point of time, for the purpose of dealing with sin, in a sacrificial death and resurrection. In Christ, the mythological pattern of the religions and the 'near misses' of Israel were once for all fulfilled in history.

The evidence for the truth of the resurrection consists of the accounts of appearances, of the Empty Tomb, and the fact of the existence of the worshipping community of the Early Church, with their revolutionary observance of Sunday instead of Saturday. But it is not possible to put together the last chapters of the four Gospels and make one consistent narrative of all their details. How many women were there? Did they come to anoint a dead body or to see the sepulchre? Was it still dark or was it at dawn? How many angels? Did the women say nothing or tell the disciples? Hence the attempts to represent the whole story as the work of the over-wrought emotions of the women and the suggestions that the body was removed either by the Romans or the Jews to forestall possible later disturbances, or in the quiet of the Sabbath by the disciples. By believers all these suggestions seem wanting in cogency.

The sceptics will always have difficulty in making out a really convincing case about the disposal of the body. If only the body could have been produced afterwards, the whole Christian movement would have been immediately stifled by its opponents.

But it will be readily conceded that in the last resort our views on the Empty Tomb will depend on our way of looking at the Bible as a whole, for historical evidence cannot of itself either disprove or prove the fact of the Resurrection. It has been well said that God does not crush his children into obedience by the sheer weight of the evidence but that those who have experienced the truth as it is in Jesus and have learned to trust God in their lives find the claim of the Church entirely credible. The statement therefore that Jesus rose again on the third day is more than a statement about Jesus: it is an act of Christian commitment, and apart from its grammar has nothing in common with a statement that on the third day someone rose from his bed.[1] Anyone could make that assertion. Only a minority can assert that Jesus rose from the dead: those who have not known Christ cannot believe. And, vice versa, those who do not believe could not know the Risen Christ. Pontius Pilate could not have been granted such a vision. 'The world,' wrote B. F. Westcott, 'could not see Christ and Christ could not—there is a divine impossibility—shew himself to the world.'

The appearances which Luke describes are evidential in character and all take place in or near Jerusalem. This does not mean that he has no knowledge of any Galilean appearances. If the parting (24.51) is the Ascension (Acts 1.9), there must be an interval of time between 24.1-43 and 44-end, and this would allow time for a visit to Galilee and a return to Jerusalem for the feast of Pentecost, as was the habit of many devout Galileans. Possibly the final charge to the eleven given in Matthew 28 was delivered on the eve

[1] Cf. I. T. Ramsey, *Religious Language*, 1957, p. 130.

of the Pentecost pilgrimage. It may have been that while
the Lord's expressed intention was that the eleven should
proceed to Galilee, where he would meet them, in the
event their frailty made necessary the revelations in the
city. Only then, when they were assured of his risen power,
do they go to Galilee (for the appearance recorded by
Matthew and by John 21). Hence the evidential character
of the Lucan appearances: Jesus breaks bread, and then
they recognize him; he eats some fish to demonstrate
that, though the body is transformed, there is a real
continuity.

The Resurrection of Christ does not amount to evidence
for man's inherent immortality. It is slightly absurd to
imagine that what happened to the unique Son of God
should necessarily happen, as a right, to all the sons of
men. The NT teaches that believers, who have been incorporated into the Risen Body of Christ, will be fully clothed
with 'bodies' appropriate to the state of existence in the
Kingdom of God; and this is a divine state of grace. Christ
is the first-fruits of the Resurrection, in the sense that what
happened to him, may, by grace, happen to those who
belong to him. And what happened to him between Good
Friday and Easter Day is what will happen to us between
death and the Last Day. The answer to the penitent thief
(23.43) probably means that he would be in the temporary
abode of the saints who await the general resurrection.
Because Christ has conquered the last enemy, death, the
Christian's baptism is a more important stage in the process of glorification than his death, which for all its horror
and unnaturalness no longer appals; it is the gateway, not
into heaven, but into a resting with Jesus, which is a state
not of passive inactivity or unconsciousness, but an incomplete state—nearer to Jesus than we are (Phil. 1.23), yet
one destined to be fulfilled only at the Parousia. No doubt
it is a state of purification.

In the NT then death does not give a welcome release

to the immortal soul, for bodies do not have discarnate immortal souls inevitably attached to them.

In the Lucan post-resurrection narratives the Lord has both preached and broken bread: so too in his Church the Risen Lord continues to be present both in the preaching of the Word and in the sacrament of the Eucharist.

THE ASCENSION

24.50-53

The Gospel's account of the Lord's departure is extremely brief and it could read as if the event, like the Resurrection, also took place 'on the third day', in agreement with the Longer Ending of Mark (a late addition to the Gospel), and perhaps also Matthew and St Paul. But this impression is corrected by Acts 1 which re-tells the story with additional information and a clear statement that there was an interval between Easter and the Ascension. In both accounts the Lord appears to the Eleven (Luke 24.44 = Acts 1.3), gives them their commission (47-48 = Acts 1.8), and then is taken into heaven. BETHANY (50) was probably on the eastern slopes of the Mount of Olives (Acts 1.12). Luke was therefore almost certainly not conscious of any contradiction between his two Ascension narratives, and an interval of time must be assumed between 24.43 and 44. It is the function of Acts 1 to make this interval explicit, and in doing so it becomes the only NT book to mention a period of forty days. Forty is a number of interest in itself and, like the number seven, is used by religions other than Judaism; but forty years or forty days is especially a period with abundant OT associations, which Luke was predisposed to use, just as he will later divide Moses' life into three periods of forty years and allot forty years to the reign of Saul (Acts 7.23, 30, 36;

13.21). But Luke's predisposition was irresistible when he recalled that Elijah once 'arose', and 'did eat and drink, and went . . . forty days and forty nights unto Horeb the mount of God' (I Kings 19.8). What happened to Elijah (he was one of the two OT personages who went not down to Sheol but up to heaven) has happened to the Lord.

The Church's first liturgical thoughts were to celebrate only the Easter festival: a later generation added Whitsun, and from the fourth century Ascension Day. From then the chronological scheme of Acts has been the liturgical norm, for which we may be grateful. To contemplate the entire process of Christ's triumph in a single festival is a far greater burden to the human mind than a dispersal of it through the moments of Good Friday, Easter Day, Ascension and Pentecost. And was the Church not wise to use the symbols of forty and fifty which have attracted the human mind so widely, and thus to teach that the anticipations of the world's religions have been at last fulfilled?

At any rate both in Luke-Acts and in the other NT writings the Ascension differs from the other Resurrection appearances. It was different in its character of finality; and it marked a deliberate change in the manner of the Lord's presence in his Church, for it was the completion of his redemptive work. Other books in the NT assume, if they do not state, a doctrine of the Ascension, which is the term used to express the passage to the state of final bliss in the Kingdom of God. Thus Revelation in ch. 11 describes the two witnesses as being killed (7), raised to life (11), and finally, 'they went up into heaven in the cloud' (12). So also I Thess. 4.16, 17. This is the full round of Christian expectation; the last term in the process of God's redeeming his universe is that in which the whole Church is brought into final relationship with himself. We must therefore see in the Ascension, 'not the transportation of an earthly frame to a localized heaven but the consummation of the process, including death and Resurrection, whereby the manhood, i.e. the human organism, of the Son of God was transformed while still retaining its identity' (J. G. Davies, *He Ascended into Heaven*, 1957, p. 146). Some theologians have thought that first-century Jews could only have been taught this by Christ if he ascended physically, and was seen to go up higher and higher; but it is more likely that, on the historical basis of a final appearance and final charge, Luke has given a theological interpretation by means of OT typology, and the conventional cloud symbolism which recalled the Transfiguration; only this time Jesus enters the cloud of the divine presence to remain there until he comes again 'in like manner' (Acts 1.11).